To Richard Wade,
with admiration and gratitude;
the first generation of graduate students
of American Studies in Yugoslavia.
Dubrovnik, October 10, 86

Borka Vučinić
Dubravka Kodela
Višnja Brcković
Silva Tomanić
Sanja Šmagjan Pavlović

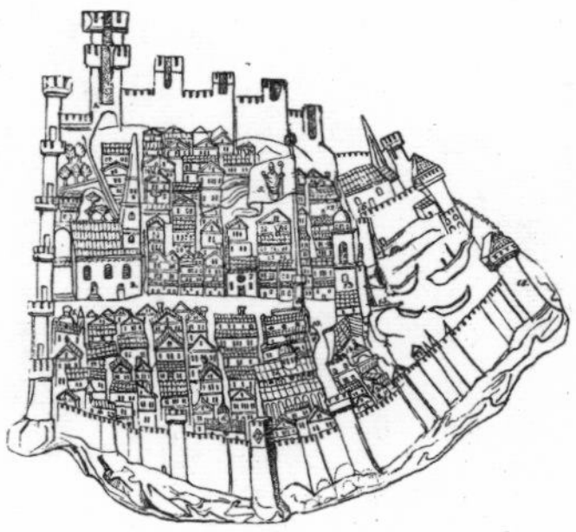

Dubrovnik

LIBRARY: MONOGRAPHS

YU ISBN 86-7133-011-7

Editorial board:

Ana Ivelja-Dalmatin
Mato Novaković
Slobodan Žalić

Editor in chief:

Katarina Milanović

Art layout:

Ivan Rožmarić

Proof reader:

Mile Maslać

For the publisher:

Pavle Nikšić

Text:

Dubravka Beritić
Rudi Jelić
Krešimir Kovačević
Mirko Kratofil
Ivo Lentić
Josip Lučić
Josip Luetić
Marija Novaković
Kruno Prijatelj
Tomo Vlahutin

Translated by:

Nikolina Jovanović

Reviews:

Josip Lučić
Anuška Novaković

Photographs:

Mato Novaković, chief photographer
Milan Babić
Tošo Dabac
Milan Pavić
Antun Tasovac
Vilko Zuber
Archive of »Turistkomerc«
Archive of Dubrovnik Summer Festival

Publisher:

»Turistkomerc«, Zagreb, Ilica 26/I

Printed in Croato-Serbian,
German, English and French

Printed by:

turistkomerc Zagreb, 1986.

Contents

*»AND SO, MY DEAREST DUBRAVA, FROM THIS LONELY,
IMMORTAL ROCK, TAKE THE GREETINGS OF A POET, THE
KISS OF A LOVER, THE BLESSING OF ONE WHO IS
FORTUNATE, BECAUSE IN THE GLORY OF THE PAST IS
BORN THE LAST DREAM OF A POET: YOUR FUTURE.«*

(Ivo Vojnović)

Under our very eyes a strong stone nest is formed, enriched by the thousands of people who live and work in it, and by the coloured feathers of the horizon of the sea and sky. Seen from the slopes of Mount Srđ, it glitters in a sea of sunlight and lapping waves, in Mediterranean vegetation, especially its famous agava cacti. Towers, belfries, churches, cathedral domes, mansions and terraces, fountains, squares and piazzas, rising garlands of houses with ancient roofs, old open-hearth kitchens and chimneys, walls, forts, fortresses, and bulwarks that have encircled the Town for millenia and are unforgettable.

Washed by the waves of thought and memory, today we stand, feet firmly planted on the old, hard paving, durable and indestructable as in days gone by. Square stone slabs washed by the steps of centuries, they are so worn by the torents of people that they are akin to a human face, which expresses all the storms of change.

Who has not cruised through the narrow streets of the Old Town, circled around to Prijeki street, entered the Town through Ruža, gone up and down winding stairways, stopped before small churches and examined portals, rose-windows, or some stone bell-cote, who has not lifted the latches of these doors, taken out keys, banged a door-knocker, and who among the poets, people of Dubrovnik and visitors, has not passed through the large town gates of Pile or Ploče and stridden joyfully or sadly across the wooden drawbridge. Who has not looked on Dubrovnik's shining dawns and mornings through narrow and quiet windows, weighted by their lintels, into days and nights full of stars, into emptiness or joy, who has not made a pilgrimage to the bulwarks, kept vigil for the enemy, sighted a rowing-boat or galleon, or the Dubrovnik fleet in full sail. We could list Dubrovnik memories: the Town of our childhood, our school days, our youth and our first flights of knowledge, the Town of our first love when the stars descended onto Stradun and dawn spun on its heel, Town of races and joy, of serenades and guitars, of calling from under windows, Town of carnivals, masquerades and masked balls, Town of our first literary Arcadia and academies, the celebrated old *Slovinac* and *Dubrovnik,* Town of spontaneous and numerous actors' companies, »Njarnjas« and »Pomet«, of colleges, the famous Collegium Ragusinum, Antunin, and much, much more.

Dubrovnik is a living mosaic of human physical and spiritual power, of everything man can leave as a lasting message and a trace of his life. Its achievements, from the first days when it was founded on ancient rocks, and during the centuries that passed over the republican state of three councils headed by a Rector, were many: a maritime merchant fleet that sailed over the whole world and at times led in Europe; a shore-based trading network that spread into neighbouring Bosnia, Herzegovina, Boka Kotorska, Montenegro, Serbia, Croatia, Macedonia, Romania, Bulgaria, all way to Constantinople and Asian and African lands; sculpters' and painters' workshops; schools, literacy, oratory, diplomacy; science and discoveries; the greatest literary and musical achievements. All these were lasting messages for humanity, the marks of a tough and characteristic Dalmatia in sunny Dubrovnik, of the Mediterranean-Adriatic existence of a free town and people, which even before the 10th century could proudly call itself *Stato Ragusea* and *Nazione Ragusea*.

Looking at the life of this Town: rocks underfoot, the mountain of Srđ behind it, craggy shores to the east and west, and in front the open sea, studded by a garland of islands and islets, we get a complete picture of the work of heroic Dubrovnik, the capabilities of its mind and the skill it needed to turn this dry, angry and rocky soil into a flowering garden of architecture and many kinds of artistic and practical beauty.

Dubrovnik is proof that the human hand can change nature, that self-denying paths of the mind, through practical application to art, can fill life with fruitful content that has a meaning for eternity.

Dubrovnik's past casts a livnig beam forward into the present, and in passing embraces us all. Old Lausa from before Christ still stands, the rock of Ragusa after Christ, tough centuries of human change in the Dubrovnik Republic, poets, scientists, scholars, musicians, builders, merchants and seamen and their houses, the Town before the earthquake and the Town after the earthquake, forts that have withstood all, even time, proud Lovrijenac jutting out on guard like a threat to Venice and all would-be conquerors, the legend of Srđ and Dubrav-ka, who descends to the sea from its breast, rocks that confront stormy waves, Porporela - the beauty of the Old Harbour, and in it the mingled chords of lutes and guitars.

It is not necessary to sing hymns of praise to the heroic past of Dubrovnik. It is only necessary to pass through the Town and witness all that took part in it during millenia.

And from this past to experience Dubrovnik today, a Town of unique beauty, the tourist metropolis of the Yugoslav coast, a Town of new urban settlements, fine modern hotels, meetings of scholars, scientists, politicians and men of culture, an international stage for the Summer Festival and for the best achievements of the theatre, a musical, artistic and cultural heritage for the world.

A town with an open heart and joyful welcome to all known and unknown friends, which lovingly offers its visitors a part of itself and its unrepeatable beauty. Finally, a Town of old glory, which in the joy of its present rapid growth and new flowering flies high the banner of liberty, the symbol of old glory and of its newly-born liberty in its free socialist homeland, Yugoslavia.

Marija Novaković

Dubrovnik Today

Ships, airplanes and buses with passengers from the whole world come here to experience unforgettable beauty, something they will wish to see again. Students on the town streets, scholars at symposiums and discussions, actors on squares and fortifications, workers in new factories, hotels and new apartments... For three decades socialism has been being built in Yugoslavia, self-managing socialism, the result of the victory of the National Liberation War and the armed revolution, through which the peoples of Yugoslavia, and its working class under the leadership of the Communist Party of Yugoslavia and Comrade Tito, laid the first foundations for the social and material transformation of Yugoslavia.

From the very first days of occupation, in 1941, based on the traditions of the workers' movement, the National Liberation Struggle for liberty and freedom from all enemies and fascist occupiers of the land developed and grew in Dubrovnik. The Dubrovnik partizan detachment was formed during the armed struggle. Later it became part of the famous Second Dalmatian Proletarian Shock Brigade, which together with the Tenth Herzegovina Brigade, freed Dubrovnik in October, 1944.

During the war National Liberation Councils were organized in several places in the Dubrovnik region (in Dubrovnik, on Pelješac, Mljet, along the Dubrovnik coast, in Župa Dubrovačka and in Konavli). They were local bodies of peoples' government, which became the nuclei of true national government. After victory and liberation those first bodies of national government merged and united into the National Liberation Council of Dubrovnik and several District National Liberation Councils, inter-connected in the Zonal National Liberation Council of Dubrovnik. After reorganization in later years, this whole region is today a single political and economic whole represented by the Assembly of the Commune of Dubrovnik. During post-war years of renewal the town of Dubrovnik became the core of the region, a position it still holds today in this period of intensive construction and development of the whole Dubrovnik region. When liberation came, the Dubrovnik economy and the social services of this region were in bad condition.

Dubrovnik's pre-war fleet, which made up almost one half of the merchant fleet of pre-war Yugoslavia, and some of whose ships sailed in Allied convoys during the war, was destroyed. Hotels and other tourist facilities were destroyed or unusable, trade small, there was hardly any industry, only two small factories.

The town started out with a badly equipped economy and infrastructure. In 1948 there were 47,515 inhabitants in the Dubrovnik region, 16,733 of whom lived in the town of Dubrovnik. Only 10 settlements were electrified. Of a total of 232 kilometres of roads, 26 kilometres were asphalted. There were several hundred beds for tourists.

It was not until the fifties that reconstruction on any considerable scale began. New premises were built for the Maritime School, which was founded in Dubrovnik in 1852 and schooled most of the crews of Dubrovnik and Yugoslav ships.

In 1953 a factory for coal-graphite products was built, which changed the economic structure, and also a small hydroelectric power station in Zavrelje - Župa Dubrovačka. The reconstruction started during those years has never ceased since. From year to year old and new Dubrovnik grow and develop.

The basic tendencies of development became the building of maritime and other communications, tourist facilities and accompanying activities, like trade and communal economy.

Great investment in communal facilities was urgent both because of the standard of the inhabitants, and for the needs of tourism. It was necessary to reconstruct the sewage system and connect the sewage and waterworks of new settlements to the Petka drainage canal on Lapad. This also made possible the building of new tourist and catering facilities.

In 1961 the first new tourist facilities started work, the airport was opened, retail trade reconstructed and two large retail organizations formed

- Budućnost and Minčeta. Most money was invested in new maritime communications.

These, and tourism, remain the two most important branches in the further economic development of the Dubrovnik region. There are plans for further investment in hotels, tourist and communal services, and services ancillary to them. The plans are long-term, but their first results are seen in the better organization and strengthening of the existing catering network.

From 1967 onwards investment, economic and noneconomic, constantly grew, especially in building of apartmets and communal facilities, in culture and education. The greatest increase in investment was recorded in 1967-1969, and in 1975 - 1976. In the 70-ties the absolute amount of the average five-year investment in the Dubrovnik region was higher than the republican and Dalmatian regional level, and in some years was fourth, fifth or sixth in the Socialist Republic of Croatia.

The Atlantska Plovidba enterprise, founded in 1955, continues Dubrovnik's rich seafaring and shipping tradition. It has an important influence on the whole development of the town, not only because of the ships and the people on them, but also because of important contributions in many spheres of town life and development - the building of apartment houses, health, schooling, sports, aid to other work organizations and Dubrovnik culture.

When the enterprise was founded 20 years ago it had 7 ships with a total of 58.477 DWT, and an average age of 35 years, propelled by steam and coal. Today it has become one of the leading Yugoslav shipping enterprises.

Dubrovnik's harbour economy is based on transshipment, chiefly of wood, bulk cargo and more and more food. Almost half a million passengers come to and leave Dubrovnik by ship. Car-ferry connections with other Adriatic ports increased the number of cars transported. Ships touring the Mediterranean and the Adriatic regularly visit the Dubrovnik port of Gruž. There is also a special marina for yachts in Rijeka Dubrovačka.

The basis of Dubrovnik's maritime economy are its qualified seamen. They are trained in the Maritime School founded in 1852, and the Higher Maritime School founded in 1959, which schools deck officers and engineers for merchant ships.

Graduates of these schools successfully command and manage ships on all seas, and also successfully work in many land jobs, in agencies, tourism etc.

Tourism takes a special place in the Dubrovnik region. Touristically Dubrovnik is one of the most attractive regions in Yugoslavia. Its tourism has much to offer, service is of high quality, and there are many kinds of accommodation. Dubrovnik's tourist development is based on the attraction of the old town with its fortifications and all the cultural and historical features of a rich past, on a temperate Mediterranean climate (average annual temperature is 16°C) and the blue, clear sea. The whole social and cultural life of Dubrovnik takes place around the old town, and the importance of the hotels is the greater the closer they are to it .

Most tourist traffic comes to the town itself, where the main hotels are situated, and to Cavtat and Župa Dubrovačka. During recent years a large number of new hotels of »B«, »A« and »de luxe« category, and tourist settlements, have been built close to and further away from the town, which shows the regular distribution of accommodation.

The hotel-tourist centre of Babin Kuk has all the characteristics of a small settlement with the necessary facilities for tourism, and with its own shopping centre. This is a new manner of provisioning hotels, and a more successful and rational way of doing business. Babin Kuk is a single hotel complex with many things to offer tourists - accommodation, food, shopping, recreation, sports and other services. There are three categories of accommodation. A hotel of »de luxe« category and three hotels of »A« category have rooms with balconies and a view of the sea, restaurants, outdoor and indoor cafes, saunas, conference halls, a casino, a small harbour, swimming-pools etc.

The shopping centre has a restaurant, pizza-parlour, coffeehouse, cake shop, wine cellar and beer-parlour, jazz club, boutiques, a bank, post-office, information and travel agency, hairdresser's salon etc.

There are sports grounds for volley-ball, basketball, skittles, tennis and table tennis.

The shopping centre plays an important role in food preparation not only for Babin Kuk, but also for the other hotels of the Hotel and Catering Enterprise Dubrovnik, and represents a turning-point in the existing manner of doing business in Dubrovnik hotels.

Babin Kuk and the main Dubrovnik hotels of »de luxe«, »A« and »B« category have all been built or enlarged during the last decade - the Belvedere had a new large wing added to it, the Argentina was enlarged. So also were the Park, Plat, Dubrovnik-Palace, Adriatik, Splendid, Lafodia and others belonging to the enterprise.

Cavtat, one of the most beautiful settlements on the Dubrovnik riviera, has begun to develop fast during recent years with the building of new hotels - Albatros, Croatia and several hotels of »B« category. Tourism has given a new aspect to its cultural and historical heritage and to its magnificent natural beauties. Changes in the quality of Cavtat tourism took place after the building of Croatia Hotel. The kind of visitors changed, the season lengthened and now lasts the whole year. There are many beds in private homes.

Tourism has also changed the agricultural Župa Dubrovačka and the coastal region. Hotels and tourist settlements were built in Mlini and Srebreno, while Kupari was completely revived.There is also socially owned accommodation in Slano, Trpanj and Lopud. The Dubrovnik region has many natural sites very favourable for future tourist development, like Mljet, Zaton, Šipan, Ston and Molunat.

There are many foreign and Yugoslav tourist agencies, leading among which is Dubrovnik Atlas, a Yugoslav travel agency. It used to be a small tourist bureau which worked chiefly in the Dubrovnik region, and today is an agency known in almost the whole tourist world. Atlas organizes the foreign sales of a large part of Adriatic accommodation, and its services are used by many Yugoslav and foreign tourists. Its comfortable buses and white fleet take tourists on excursions in the Dubrovnik region and abroad by boat or 'plane.

Other agencies are also included in Dubrovnik's tourist development (Jugotours, Kompas, Generalturist etc.). As tourism developed in Dubrovnik, the Hotel School Centre was founded, which includes a Catering School with practical training, a School for Highly-qualified Workers in Catering, a School for Qualified Workers and a School for Hotel Hostesses. The Libertas and Lero Hotels and the Jadran Restaurant are also part of the Centre and are used in schooling. Almost all those employed in Dubrovnik hotels since 1947 were schooled in the Centre.

Highly qualified employees are trained in the Higher Tourist School and at the Faculty for Tourism and External Trade in Dubrovnik.

The building of Dubrovnik Airport contributed to the expansion of tourism in the Dubrovnik region and in the southern Adriatic. It gave Dubrovnik another »window into the world« and enabled new tourists, from distant parts of the world, to come there.

The airport (20 kilometres from the town, 4 kilometres from Cavtat and 8 kilometres from Župa Dubrovačka) has kept abreast of all new achievements and changes in air traffic, and is capable of landing all types of aircraft in traffic today. The Dubrovnik airport provides services for 30 Yugoslav and foreign air companies and about 900,000 passengers land and take off from it.

Retail trade is also part of tourism. Dubrovnik supplies its inhabitants and tourists in many beautiful, well arranged and well provisioned shops. There are also the large shops and department stores of the »Dubrovkinja« firm.

Dubrovnik still retains its traditional role as a centre of trade not only in Yugoslavia, but also in imports and exports. The Dubrovnik market is supplied from the whole of Yugoslavia. Today, as before, Dubrovnik has remained a town open to producers from the whole of Yugoslavia and a great number of firms from various parts of the country have their shops there. Most shops in the old part of the town are geared to the needs of tourists (shops selling goldwork and filigrees, handicrafts and other specialized shops).

Industry does not play a great role in the economic structure of Dubrovnik. However, although small in scope, Dubrovnik's industry is productive and has done a lot in the foundation of new plants. There are several factories. The first Dalmatian industrial enterprise Radeljević (it bears the name of a Dubrovnik revolutionary) produces olive and plant oils and tallow, stearin acids and olein. Today this factory is part of the Zagreb Oil Factory.

The Nikola Mašanović factory of coal and graphite products (the name of a Dubrovnik revolutionary) is the largest industry in Dubrovnik, and the only of its kind in Yugoslavia. It produces electrographite blocks, dynamo brushes, metal stands, low-percentage graphites, contacts, electrographites, brushes and other parts for diezel and electric locomotives. A new plant has been built in Rijeka Dubrovačka.

The Dubravka paint factory produces oil paints, laquers, synthetic enamel, marine paints etc., and exports some of its products. Its production is highly profitable on a European level, so that it is one of the leading factories of its kind in Yugoslavia.

Dalmacijabilje buys, processes and exports aromatic plants and etheric oils, and its work is connected with the mountainous part of the commune (the buying of herbs). Part of the Saponia Factory in Osijek, it also produces cosmetics. Its activities also include buying, processing and exporting mushrooms and processing snails.

The Dubrovnik hydro-electric power station is one of the giants of the Yugoslav power system. It is part of the hydro-electric system on the river Trebišnjica. The Grančarevo and Gorica dams formed reservoirs, and a 17 kilometre long tunnel brings water to the Dubrovnik power station in Plat.

Elektrojug distibutes electric energy, and is constantly investing in the modernization of the low-voltage electric network, transformer stations and long-distance power cables. Thanks to the efforts of this work organization the Dubrovnik region has been completely electrified.

Immigration and natural population increase have created an acute housing problem in the Dubrovnik region. At the end of the fifties socially owned apartment housses started to be built, and building firms started to mechanize and obtain equipment for building high-rises. The system of financing was improved. Today building is directed by the Institute for the Construction of Dubrovnik. Dubrovnik has the following new settlements: Batala, Montovierna north, Montovierna south, Hladnice, Kono, Mokošica, Gorica and Gruž-Srđ, and one in Župa Dubrovačka, called Dubrovnik II.

Several building organizations and smaller crafts firms cooperate in building. Graditelj Constructors, now celebrating its 30th anniversary, and Dubac Constructors united into a large construction enterprise called Dubrovnik. In past years Dubrovnik's construction enterprises have taken part in large building undertakings: parts of the Zagreb - Karlovac freeway, parts of the Adriatic Coast Road, the Bosnia Highway, the flyover crossing at Opuzen, the airport, and almost all Dubrovnik's hotels, housing developments and a large number of its factories.

Services are laid on for a town twice the size of Dubrovnik, because they must meet double capacity during the main tourist season.

Public transport is organized by the Libertas firm, and there is a taxi-service.

Dubrovnik's postal, telephone and telegraph service are at European level. Almost every household in the town region has a telephone, and the PTT service is spreading outside the town. Dubrovnik is included in the automatic Yugoslav and European telegraph-telephone, teleprinter network.

Agriculture in the Dubrovnik region is Mediterranean in type, growing grapes, fruit, vegetables and flowers on not very fertile soil scattered in small holdings. Recently it has gone through qualitative changes. The production of wine has increased, and also fruit and vegetables. Motorcultivators and tractors have squeezed out horses and mules, and taken the place of many human hands.

There are socially-owned agricultural estates Agrum and Rudine, cooperatives and wine-cellars were formed in Potomje, Janjina, Putnikovići, Ston, Komolac and Gruda. The Dubrovnik region also produces the famous and first Yugoslav protected wines Dingač and Postup, highquality Malvazija and others.

Individual holdings get credits for cooperation with socially-owned estates.

Today only 25% of all the inhabitants live in the village, and only 10% are active in agriculture. Agricultural production partially supplies the Dubrovnik market with vegetables and meat, and there is a surplus of wine.

After the road from Ston to Orebić and Trpanj was built, and after electrification, the Pelješac peninsula revived. Individual agricultural holdings grow wine on a cooperative basis. In some places small industrial plants such as the Plamet factory were built (in Pijavičina), there is a bakery in Kuna, salt-flats in Ston, a hotel in Trpanj, and in Trpanj, Žuljani, Trstenik, Prapratno and Ston tourism is developed in private homes.

Konavle is a region of green, tilled fields, which since the building of the tunnel are no longer regularly flooded. The region has gone through a period of rapid development. Its hard-working inhabitants supply Dubrovnik, and other large consumer centres in Yugoslavia, from their model tilled holdings. The basis of production is the Agrum factory-farm with wine-cellars, dairy, slaughter-house and bakery. It also owns the famous excursion spot and restaurant Konavoski Dvori and Molunat, a future tourist settlement. The whole region is famous for its lovely national costume. It guards its cultural heritage and original folk dances and is becoming touristically very attractive, so that tourism, especially excursionist tourism, is more and more important in Konavli.

Here, in Čilipi, the modern Dubrovnik Airport was built, which has contributed greately to general development. First in the Dubrovnik archipelago is the green island of Lokrum, the nearest and most famous excursion spot and beach for Dubrovnik people. Then there are the Elaphite Islands, where tourism is being developed. Lopud has magnificent vegetation, well-tended parks and lovely shingle beaches with modern hotels, while the tranquil and picturesque Koločep and Šipan are islands of future tourist development.

Mljet is the longest among them. It has a national park of indescribable beauty, with woods and lakes, Melita Hotel on an island in the middle of a large lake, and awaits future tourist development.

Dubrovnik plays a very important role in culture, education, schooling, scholarship, art, science, health, society and sports. In the best days of the Dubrovnik Republic seafaring and trade made great profits, so that public buildings to serve the Republic, its state functions and defense were built. That old inner part of the town inside the excellently preserved town walls still stands, with its forts of Lovrijenac, Revelin, Bokar and Sveti Ivan, well-planned streets, churches and civic and communal facilities (waterworks and sewage). It is a great cultural and historical treasure, the backbone around which the whole social life of Dubrovnik has taken place. Dubrovnik's cultural heritage became the basis for further economic and social development. Its tourism developed on the basis of its cultural heritage, and cultural activities depend on tourism. The Summer Festival is based on the urban harmony of the town, the theatre and the orchestra, but neither the theatre nor orchestra, nor Linđo, would be what they are without the Summer Festival, without tourism.

The several old cultural institutions (Regional Museum founded in 1872, formerly in Sveti Ivan, the Archives dating from 1920, formerly in the Rector's Palace and the Philharmonic) have today grown into a score of cultural and scholarly institutions, and there are also many cultural and historical monuments. The Sponza, Revelin, Bokar and other buildings, today used for culture, were not used for such purposes before. A socialist approach to the cultural heritage was reflected in the enthusiasm with which the renewal of cultural and historical monuments was started. New institutions were founded. The Art Gallery, in a lovely building in Ploče with ample exhibition space and a lovely view of the old town, has a large stock of paintings (19th and 20th century) and regularly organizes exhibitions by Dubrovnik and Yugoslav painters. It also has a valuable collection of sculptures including the works of Meštrović, Kršinić, Lozica, Radovani, Džamonja, Ružić, Radauš, Mitrović, Kocković, Vulas and others, and also a valuable collection of over 300 icons from the 16th to the 19th centuries

In the old town there is also the Sebastijan Gallery organized by the Atlas Agency, close to the Dominican Monastery, and the Božidarević Gallery

on Trg oružja. The atriums of the Theatre and the Trade Unions Building are also sometimes used for art exhibitions, and with the restoration of the Lazaret a valuable new exhibition site was obtained.

The Orthodox church has old 15th to 19th century icons. Dubrovnik's modern artistic life is rich and is represented by about 20 artists. In Cavtat there is the Bukovac Gallery with paintings by Cavtat-born Vlaho Bukovac. The Commune Library was founden in 1947 and has a rich and valuable stock of scientific books from Dubrovnik's past. Later it got the name Scholarly Library. Until 1975 it was situated in the Rector's Palace, and today is in the Skočibuha Mansion in Boninovo.

The Marin Držić Theatre continues the traditions of Dubrovnik's theatre acting companies and regularly performs at the Dubrovnik Summer Festival from its repertoire of Dubrovnik literature. It has been awarded several valuable acknowledgements, and so have also some of its members. The theatre building was built in 1863, and its ceiling decorated by Vlaho Bukovac at the end of the 19th century. The Dubrovnik Summer Festival is the most important Yugoslav cultural event, held in July and August. It impinges on all other cultural institutions and gives its mark to the town during that period.

The town orchestra holds concerts the whole year round, and is greatly esteemed for its performances at the Dubrovnik Summer Festival. There is a constant influx of new musicians from among the pupils of the Music School, and there is also a department of the Music Academy of Zagreb in Dubrovnik.

Several musicians,, and some famous pop groups, work in Dubrovnik, like the Dubrovački Trubaduri, the Dubrovački Poklisari and the Maestral group.

The Dubrovnik folklore group Linđo has now existed for 10 years and presents Dubrovnik and Yugoslav folk dances.

The richness and power of the Dubrovnik Republic can be seen in many town museums. The Rector's Palace houses the Cultural and Historical

Museum with valuable exhibits from the Republic's public and political life. The Fort of Sveti Ivan houses the Ethnographic Museum with exhibits from the territory of the Dubrovnik Republic. The Rupe Museum, where wheat was stored during the Republic, has archaeological and ethnographic exhibits. On the ground floor of the Divona (Sponza) Mansion is the Museum of the Socialist Revolution, with documents from the development of the workers' movement in Dubrovnik and from Dubrovnik's and Dalmatia's struggles during the National Liberation War. The Maritime Museum shows the rich and tempestous history of Dubrovnik seafaring. The Rector's Palace also has a collection from the 1420 Domus Christi pharmacy. The other pharmacy, founded in 1317 and one of the oldest in Europe, is in the Franciscan Monastery.

The Historical (Dubrovnik) Archives, housed in one of the most beautiful mansions, the Sponza, are an inexhaustible source for studying the history of Dubrovnik and the surrounding Balkan states. They have very valuable exhibits. In 1960 Dubrovnik got an Institute for the Preservation of Cultural Monuments and Natural Beauties, an institution which pays great attention to the preservation of monuments and cultural treasures.

Several institutes of the Yugoslav Academy of Sciences and Arts are active in Dubrovnik: the Maritime Institute with the Maritime Museum, the Historical Institute in the Sorkočević Villa on Lapad, the Institute for Corrosion and Desalinization in the Monastery of St. Jacob and the Biological Institute in the Fort of Sveti Ivan with an Aquarium and Natural History Museum on Lokrum. In Trsteno is the famous Arboretum Park, protected as the largest park of exotic plants in Yugoslavia.

The media are represented by the Dubrovnik Radio-television Centre, part of Radio-television Zagreb, and the *Dubrovački vjesnik,* a weekly of the Dubrovnik Socialist Alliance of Working People. A cultural periodical *Dubrovnik* is also published, a periodical for maritime activities *Naše More,* and *Laus,* a youth paper.

The speed of social and political development, the socialist character of economy and a socialist approach to education resulted in the organization of a widespread network of elementary education. On the territory of the Dubrovnik commune there are 15 elementary schools with 65 local departments of the lower forms. New schools were built in Lapad, Gruž, Orašac, Ston, Slano, Babino polje, Župa, Gruda and elsewhere, and the transport of pupils to schools organized. The pre-school network includes 40% children and is one of the largest in Yugoslavia. Secondary schooling is geared to the needs of the economy and social services. Thus there is the Maritime School with a nautical and engineering department, Economic School, Bussines School and a Music School. Since 1959 there has been a Higher Maritime School with a nautical and engineering department, a Higher Tourist School and, since recently, a Higher Teahcers' Training College. The Faculty for External Trade and Tourism has existed since 1969 and it teaches students from Dubrovnik and the wider surrounding region.

Post-graduate studies are organized in several branches in Dubrovnik by Zagreb Universy, and the Inter-University Centre attracts scholars from the whole world at symposiums concerning various activities and problems.

Dubrovnik has grown into an important medical centre with a well-organized health serrvice. Today's hospital building was erected in 1888, and before that the Lazaret was used for contageous diseases, and the Nuncijata for mental diseases. The development of Dubrovnik's health service started directly after liberation when the number of beds was increased, new departments founded, and also specialist surgeries, supplementary medical units, dispensaries, first-aid centres in all the larger settlements of the commune, dentistries etc. The health service has a sufficient number of doctors and a large number of nurses. Since 1959 there has been a Nursing School, which has contributed to the progress of the medical service. Today 99% children are born in hospital, ten years ago the figure was 64%.

With regard to the increased number of inhabitants and those socially insured, a new hospital is being built in Medarevo, on Lapad. This will create a new basis for the further development of the health service.

The traddition of charitable aid, especially for children (the orphanage) and the old, poor and infirm (Domus Christi), introduced during the Dubrovnik Republic, has been continued until today, and is one of the most highly developed social services in the Socialist Republic of Croatia. In Dubrovnik there is the Home for the Social Protection of Adults, an Old-age Pensioners' Hostel and a Children's Home, Ivo Vukušić.

Inhabitants and tourists alike demand more and more space for sports and recreation, and new sports grounds are planned. The young play various sports, but water sports are the most popular: water-polo, swimming, sailing, rowing and underwater fishing. In all of them fine results have been achieved. Several sites for sports grounds and halls have been planned on the territory of Dubrovnik, the most important being Gospino polje on Lapad, where a sports-recreation centre is to be built.

Since 1969 Dubrovnik has had a Regional Plan, on the basis of which many detailed plans have been made. The Regional Town Plan Includes the region from Brsečine in the west, to Čilipi in the east.

Spatial development foresees three basic zones: 1. the central part of the town from Orsula to Kantafiga and Rijeka Dubrovačka; 2. the western zone from Rijeka Dubrovačka to Brsečina, with the islands of Koločep and Lopud; 3. the eastern zone to Čilipi, including Župa.

The development and results to date have made it possible to keep ahead of the average development of the Socialist Republic of Croatia, and many developed centres.

Rudi Jelić

»IF YOU ARE LOOKING FOR HEAVEN ON EARTH GO TO DUBROVNIK!«

(BERNARD SHAW)

Dubrovnik on an old post-card from 1921.
Hymns and epics have been dedicated to this liberty-loving town.
For centuries it bore the flag of hope for all those who were enslaved.
Its banner of freedom fluttered proudly on Orlando's Pillar
not only for Dubrovnik, but for all humanity.

»Oh glorious Dubrovnik, in the green grove,
our homes still stand. ivv entwined.«

(*Shepherds (Pastir)*, Vetranić, 16th century)

The church of the patron of Dubrovnik
St. Blasius: the statue of St. Blasius –
gilded silver, 15th century.

All the eyes of Dubrovnik were turned to this harbour. A maritime town, for
centuries one of the first in the Mediterranean,
its inhabitants sailed to this rock in ancient history, and turned to the sea,
to live and flourish in maritime existence.
Through this sea gate strong Dubrovnik merchant fleets came and went,
to sail the Mediterranean and the whole world.
All Dubrovnik's fortune was made in the harbour. Even in the tragic days of the
earthquake, the only hope left to this town was
its undamaged merchant fleet, sailing far-off seas.

Dubrovnik – the town resisted the centuries and still stands strong and beautiful, full of life and joy, on its rock turned to sun, sea and liberty...

The high roofs of the old town are impressive. Since olden days they have been called *kupijerte,* and have survivied people and time.

The northern circle of walls and outer walls with Minčeta Tower, that finest of Dubrovnik's towers.

The sun-burnt face of the stone Gate of Ploče, surrounded by palms, agava cacti, oleanders and green laurel, smiles gently as in days of old at anyone crossing the hearth of friendship.

The famous Dubrovnik Stradun, whose real name is
Placa, is the favourite promenade for pupils,
students, Dubrovnik citizens and visitors from the
whole world.

Here is Sponza Palace, built by the mind and work of Paskoje Miličević between
1516 and 1520. In it was the customs (Divona), mint, armoury,
Academia dei Concordi, school, in it worked the school rectors Ilija Crijević

No one should miss a walk down Stradun, because it is like missing a central experience of the whole town. Today we look through the biforium by the Luža at the many-coloured crowds milling on Stradun, instead of the guards and admirals of olden times.

The eastern opart of the town – government buildings. We look at their faithful domes, bells, and roofs in the dusk.

Orlando's Pillar was erected in 1428 and symbolizes the old merchant town and the heroic defense of Dubrovnik against the Saracens in the 9th century.

Dubrovnik - Stradun in 1912

Dubrovnik

The church of the town patron St. Blasius. It took almost 150 years for the old Romanesque-Gothic church to be built on this site. It was fimished at the end of the 15th century, damaged in the 1667 earthquake, and then in 1706 by fire. Today's baroque church was built according to plans by Marino Gropelli between 1709 and 1714. Every February Dubrovnik holds

A new baroque Cathedral was built in 1713 on the site of the old Romanesque one, which was lost in the earthquake. In it are works by Palma Giovane, Parmigianino, Salviati, a Flemish triptych, one by Titian and the *Madonna della Seggiola.* It also has one of the richest treasuries in Yugosalavia, with master-pieces of old Dubrovnik goldwork.

◁ Cathedral treasury – Reliquary head of St. Blasius shaped like the crown of Byzantine emperors 12th c. medallions.

◁ Cathedral treasury – reliquary of the Holy cross, gilded silver, 16th c., by the Dubrovnik master-craftsman Jerolim Matov.

◁ Cathedral treasury – Reliquary hand of St. Blasius shaped like an imperial glove with 12th c. medallions.

◁ Cathedral treasury – Reliquary foot of St. Blasius, gilded silver, 1684.

This gold and filigree art in the wonderful treasury of Dubrovnik Cathedral also
shows how much man can sacrifice to goodness and the
creation of beauty. Pride fills us at the thought that all this treasure of hand,
eye, heart and fine metal was created here, on Dubrovnik soil,
and that nothing was wrested from other nations.

Virgin and Child – Madonna della Seggiola, ascribed to Raphael or his school.
In the Cathedral Treasury.

The western porch of the Rector's Palace. ▷
A peaceful and harmonious ▷
creation of stone arches.

*»By chance my thoughts strayed to old Greek Madonnas who, lit by rare
wax candles in the darkness of churches, seem alive, mysterious, so
obscure are their features in the darkness of the sanctuary.«*

Geranium, Ivo Vojnović

Virgin and Child (13th century) from the church of St. Andrew in Pile,
today in the Cathedral treasury.

Capital with putti from the western porch of the Rector's Palace. The magnificent, sunny and harmonious Renaissance and the goddess of spring take poetry away from us. That is why Dinko Ranjina, Dubrovnik poet and seven times Rector in this palace, **writes**

»Oh much loved stone...
the soft pilow for my head, my pure gold,
and the sweet reward for all my efforts.«

The Rector's Palace, the Rector's work cabinet with a painting by Mihajlo Hamzić, *The Baptism of Christ.*

Rector's Palace – Paris Bordone (1500–1571), *Venus and Adonis.*

The Rector's Palace: painting of St. Blasius, by an unknown artist. In his hand the patron holds ancient Dubrovnik, which shows us what the town looked like before the eartquake.

Rector's Palace (15th century) – Cabinet (17th century).

The atrium of the Rector's Palace and the staircase leading to the halls of the Great and Small Councils, where the most important decisions about the fate of the Dubrovnik Republic were made. The worthy Dubrovchanin Miho Pracat got the most prominent place in the atriumn of this palace.

This dome that rises above the church nave could tell the moving storey of the Cathedral. With it Dubrovnik grew, was destroyed, and grew again.

Onofrio's Small Fountain is a pearl of 15th c. architecture and of the skill of its builder Onofrio de la Cava. Water brought here from the source of Dubrovnik's rivier Ombla still runs out of the same satyrs' mouths.

Prijeko – a many-coloured meeting-place of happy faces.

The old part of the town is a special experience, especially the long, dark stone-paved streets, many with hundreds of stairs, some vaulted or with arches or roofed by balconies.

Prijeko is a street of special charm whose elegant façades are adorned with rose windows, escutcheons and lacy balconies.

When Onofrio de la Cava built this small fountain in 1440, there were no pigeons. Today pigeons are the most thirsty and the most beautiful decoration of this lovely fountain.

The monument to the greatest poet of Dubrovnik, Dživo F. Gundulić, in the square that bears his name (by Rendić – 1893). These verses are the motto of the whole life of this courageous and brave republic:

»Oh beautiful, oh dear, oh sweet liberty,
the gift in which the Holy Father gave us all treasures,
the true cause of all our glory,
the only ornament of this Dubrovnik...«

The Dominican Monastery and church with bell-tower (15th
century) is the richest treasury of Dubrovnik painting, collected
during centuries and guarded by the Dominican monks.

The Romanesque-Gothic southern portal of the Dominican Church is by the sculptor Bonino di Milano.

The Gothic-renaissance cloister of the Dominican Monastery is the most precious and most beautiful part of the monastery complex. It has a rectangular base and three-light arcades. The Venetian Gothic style came to luxurious expression in the picturesque central courtyard with a stone well surrounded by fraggrant orange trees.

The Annunciation, Nikola Božidarević (15th century) in the
Dominican Museum.

Triptych by Miho Hamzić (1512) in the Dominican Museum.

Polyptych by Lovro M. Dobričević, from 1448, kept in the Museum of the Dominican Monestery. The central composition on the polyptych is *The Baptism,* while the most beautiful details of this lovely decoration are the figure of the melancholy and gentle Virgin surrounded by a mandorla of cobalt-blue angels, and the elegant figure of St. Michael.

Through this glowing stone eye we watch dusk fall on the old Dubrovnik harbour and its
protector, the dignified Fort of sv. Ivan, which was built between 1552 and 1557 by joining the
old fort of the same name and Mulo Tower. Today it holds the Aquarium, and the Maritime and
Ethnographic Museums, the invaluable treasure of Dubrovnik's cultural and maritime heritage.
One of the greatest Dubrovnik 15th century architects, Paskoje Miličević, left the imprint of his
skill on the harbour fortifications.

The irresistible Stradun, the promenade of all who are in love with this town, centuries of people walking and running, old roofs, the tireless *zelenci* striking the hours and centuries, bells whose sound scatters like pearls from the shore and the belltower. ▷

Franciscan Monastery: southern portal – *Pietà*, a work of exceptional artistic value by the Petrović brothers, 1498. ▷

Dubrovnik's web of narrow, shady, stone streets is part of its century-old past.
Here the old and the new intertwine, the unique beauty and miraculous harmony
created by skilled and gifted master-builders.

The Franciscan Church is an outstanding cultural monument with a lovely and intricate stone belltower.

The Franciscan Monastery, the lower cloister, by Miho Brajkov from Bar, 1360. The capitals on a double row of columns are each different from its neighbour. They bear many motifs from the plant, animal and human world. Whoever enters, walks around this stone porch, around these columns, several times, caught by the power of subtle stone, and gives himself up to thought.

Franciscan pharmacy in the Monastery of the
Little Brothers, one of the oldest in Europe,
founded in 1317, with original old utensils and
equipment for making medicines.

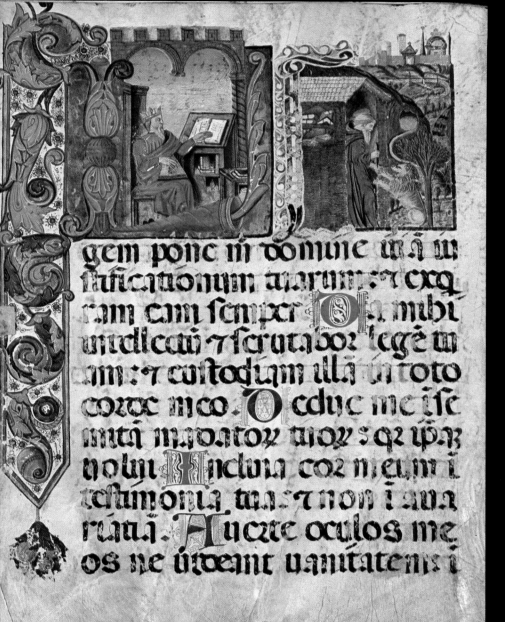

Franciscan Monastery:
detail from the polyptych
by Lovro Dobričević
(1455–1458). The figure of
St. Blasius.

Franciscan Monastery: old Library.

This lovely church of the Holy Saviour has existed since 1520. It has a votive inscription.

Facing it is Onofrio's Large Fountain, built by the famous onofrio de la Cava in 1446. From its lovely stone spouts, decorated with leaves and sunny heds, clear river water still runs.

Church of St. Spas – Stone rose window. Onofrio's Large Fountain – detail: stone satyrs. Dubrovnik's and foreign architects built this town with special love, with that singular harmony of the noble and the simple, and with especially beautiful stone sculptures.

Baroque staircase called By the Jesuits, leading to the Jesuit church. By the church the celebrated Collegium Ragusinum tells of old and new days.

The main façade of the Jesuit church of St. Ignatius.

At the bottom of the eastern wing of Prijeko street stands a pre-Romanesque church St. Nicholas the 11th century, with a mannerist façade.

There are ancient houses almost everywhere, chapels inside houses, and small churches, like this one of St. Roch.

Triptych by Nikola Božidarević in the Dance church (15th – 16th century). The wonderful painting by this local artist is impressive.

◁ The western town entrance – the Pile Gate with a stone bridge and the statue of St. Blasius.

Minčeta – Its monumental and harmonious stone still dominates the town. These bulwarks were the throne, protection and guardian of liberty, defying anyone who would raise a hand against it. Minčeta Tower guards the memory of many and famous builders, including the greatest Croatian 15th century Renaissance architect Juraj Dalmatinac.

This drawbridge leading to the Gate of Ploče was lifted when enemies approached, but lowered to greet friends, offering them goodness and harmonious shelter.

Before us lies a stone nest ennobled by thousands of its inhabitants and architects. It glitters in the sea of sun and playful ripples that lap against the stone rocks of Lokrum, an islet of romantic beauty. Who would dream that under the green roof of the islet hides the ancient Benedictine Monastery, fragrant parks, gentle beaches and bays.

No place in the town has been more bathed in waves, song and guitar music than Porporela – the faithful guardian and break-water of the old town harbour. Travellers, sailors, fishermen and Dubrovnik captains were awaited and met here, farewells said and kerchiefs waved. Porporela is still the favourite of lovers in nights when the sea embraces the starry sky.

In olden days Dubrovnik boats were ideals of skill and perfect craftsmanship. They could carry a lot, were enduring and manoeuvrable at sea. This largest ship, which could sail on all seas, is only one of the great 16th century marchant fleet.

Lovrijenac and its cannon.

Thanks to these unconquerable rocks and fortifications, Dubrovnik's adversaries during centuries, the Venetians, and many others, were often forced to turn back from under the walls of Dubrovnik having achieved nothing and with no booty.

Harmonious Bokar does not resemble a fort here, but is more like a dance
in stone of the rotonda above Kolorina, which it guards.

As if the rectors had returned, the councellors and days gone by. From Orlando's Pillar, just as they once were, the proclamations of the Rector and the Senate are read. Doves of peace are let free, Gundulić's Dubravka comes riding in a splendid cart, symphony music rings out, muskets shoot, many beautiful costumes from Konavle, Župa and Primorje intermix, the old clock strikes the night hours, and Orlando, his century-long peace broken, watches...

Franciscan Monestery: interior of church. A concert during the Dubrovnik Summer Festival.

»What can bring to life better than music the wild, magnificent poetry of the struggle between life and death, either in nature, or in a tormented soul?«.

Ekvinocij, Ivo Vojnović

Gruž – old Gravosia, today Dubrovnik's modern port, an economic and merchant centre, with modern housing developments on the forested peninsula of Lapad.

The lovely Renaissance Sorkočević Mansion in Lapad. From this family came many of Dubrovnik's poets and learned men.

The glittering sea, and the sunbeaten and wind-swept rocks of Lapad provide the setting for the Babin Kuk Hotel Complex – a paradise attracting numerous tourists who leave here with its memory forever in their hearts.

Rijeka Dubrovačka (Dubrovnik River), part of the Marina. From it water ran into Dubrovnik's fountains. The pure springwater, bays and the mountains protecting it from the wind, fertile fields on the left and right bank of Rijeka Dubrovačka. There were many settlements here, and many settlements here, and many of Dubrovnik's most beautiful summer mansions.

Ston with 14th century salt flats. After Dubrovnik the best-fortified town of the Dubrovnik Republic. Its defense towers and walls still stand.

This interesting pre-Romanesque church of St. Michael on Ston's peak dates from the 11th century.

Zaton – a lovely and picturesque settlement on the coast near Dubrovnik.

Slano is a picturesque little town of the Dubrovnik Riviera, with a long cultural tradition and numerous monuments.It lies in a lovely bay with a beautiful beach, thick pine woods and olive groves.

In order to protect its estate, Pelješac and its precious salt-works, the Republic had stone walls built on the Ston isthmus, connecting the fortified small towns of Mali and Veliki Ston. The narrow alleys, beautiful buildings, and the walls with their towers and bastions, still lure with their eternal charm.

Astarea – Dubrovačka Župa: in past times the flower garden of the townspeople of Epidaurus, and of the Dubrovnik Republic; today this is the park of the Dubrovnik Riviera, a wondrous string of modern hotels, villas, resorts, beaches orchards and flower beds, welcoming all visitors with its sunshine and fragrance.

Here we are in ancient Epidaurum (7 c.B.C.), today thriving and lovely Cavtat, a small town with many monuments of culture and history and precious works of art, like this masterpiece by the Croatian sculptor Ivan Meštrović – the Mausoleum of the Račić Family.

A moment of folk music from Konavle, from the lovely »valley with the most beautiful costume and loveliest women«. This man is playing Konavle music on bagpipes. Dressed in the ceremonial costume of his greatgrandfathers, over three hundred years old, with lively colours and motifs, he shows only part of the rich cultural and historical heritage of Konavle.

inhabitants of Konavle dance the *potkolo*. Old and young men of Konavle play fiddles, bagpipes, *gusle* and *tamburice*.

The fertile plane of Konavle with its extensive vineyard plantations stretches at the foot of Mount Sniježnica.

A natural feature are the Veliko and Malo Jezero (Large and Small Lake), formed from sea-water and submarine fresh water. This islet of sv. Marija wrote much of Mljet's cultural history; it is enough just to open the book of buildings and traces of human habitation. This Benedictine Monastery with a 12th century. Romanesque church has been so well and beautifully adapted (without spoiling any of its anicient features) into Melita Hotel. Walking around Mljet we could discover traces of the nymph Calypso and the pines whose beauty and strength hid the sky, from which Odysseus built a ship to return to Ithaca.

The History of Dubrovnik

Dubrovnik holds a special, one might even say a magnificent, place in the history of Yugoslavia. It is exceptional, it is unique and it has left a lasting mark not only on Croatian history, but on the history of all the South Slav peoples.

In ancient times the Illyrians inhabited the barren and rocky islet, really a peninsula, under Mount Srđ, and named it Ragusium. In the 2nd century B.C. a small group of Roman soldiers settled near by. The Illyrians gave the town its name, the Romans left traces and fragments of sarcophagi, inscriptions, buildings, arms.

In the 7th and 8th centuries new arrivals built the magnificent cathedral whose foundations-ruins were discovered in 1981. It had lovely 9th century frescoes (The preserved walls with frescoes have been conserved and are open to the public).

Not far from Ragusium, several miles to the south-east, flourished the Roman town-colony Epidaurum, today Cavtat. Epidaurum was a rich town, with a port, ships, buildings, trade, a water-system, crafts, organized administration and a religious community.

At the beginning of the 7th century A.D. the political and ethnic picture of the Balkans changed. The Slavs came from the north and north-east, crossed the Danube and the Sava, destroyed the old Roman towns, and permenently settled the region from the Karavan Alps to the Adriatic, the Black and Aegean Seas. This whole region they wrested from Byzantium, the heir to the old Roman Empire in that part of the Balkans.

Survivors from Epidaurum (and also some from Salona) moved to and found shelter on the rock of Ragusium, which, in 614 A.D., became the nucleus of the medieval town of the same name. Since the 12th century the new town of Ragusium has also been known under the Croatian name of Dubrovnik, which was to survive.

The new town was first mentioned in the 7th century, when an unknown geographer from Ravenna wrote: *Epidaurum, id est Ragusium* (Epidaurum is today Dubrovnik). Thus was the medieval world informed that from the ashes of the nearby ruins of Epidaurum a new settlement, a new town, had been built.

Local chronicles and annals record the beginning of that new community. But for reliable data about Dubrovnik, and also about the beginnings of other Dalmatian towns, we must turn to the Byzantine Emperor Constantine Porphyrogenitus (913-959) in his work *De administrando imperio (On Ruling the Empire)*. He describes how old Epidarium was destroyed, how the survivors managed to save themselves by hiding on the steep slopes of today's Dubrovnik, and how the settlement spread and was surrounded by walls. Security was provided for the new settlement by rugged rocks to the south and a marshy inlet to the north, which separated it from the mainland spurs of Mount Srđ. At first glance the steep and naked rock, except as a protection from attack from land and sea, did not offer any perspectives for economic progress. But the inhabitans of old Dubrovnik managed to overcome natural handicaps. Their small, newly born fishing and seafaring settlement gradually spread. The original core extending from Zaton to Cavtat was surrounded by a ring of islands (Šipan, Lopud, Koločep, Sv. Andrija, Daksa, Lokrum, Supetar, Mrkan and Bobara), and smaller islets and rocks. Neighbouring regions were gradually added: Lastovo in the middle of the 13th century; Ston and Pelješac in 1333; Mljet in the middle of the 14th century; the upper parts of Župa and Šumet in 1357; Primorje in 1399; Konavle between 1415 and 1427. With these territorial additions Dubrovnik finally extended into a small city a state, stretching from Klek to Sutorina.

During the first centuries of its history Dubrovnik lived under the protection of Byzantium (from 614 to 1205).

The other Dalmatian towns were at that time also under the same distant, and thus not very rigorous control of Bytantium. Those towns, together with Dubrovnik, formed a single political and administrative unit whose centre was in Zadar. The other Dalmatian towns changed masters during the centuries, but Dubrovnik, except for short interruptions

during the 11th and 12th centuries when it recognized the protetction of the Normans, was more or less
continuoustly under Byzantium.

From the 7th to the 9th century little is in fact
known of its history. In the 9th century the Arabs-Sa-
racens made forays into the Adriatic. Many towns
and ports on both sides of the Adriatic experienced
the fury of their sieges, sacking and conquest. In
866-867 Dubrovnik resisted a Saracen siege which
lasted for 15 months, showing that it was already
fortified by strong walls and defended by a navy.
After the siege the inhabitants of Dubrovnik continued to resist the Saracens. In 869 their boats
carried Croatian and other Slav troops to free Bari
from Saracen occupation. In several sea battles in
the 9th century the Saracens had vanquished and
destroyed much of the Venetian fleet, so that at that
time the Dubrovnik, Croatian and Neretva navies
were the strongest in the Adriatic, and the true
masters of the Adriatic, open sea and trade routes.
This was the time when the Venetians called the
Croatian Prince Domagoj (864-878) the »worst Croatian prince« (pessimus Sclavorum dux) because of
the defeats they suffered at his hands. During the
reign of Prince Branimir (879-892) they dared not
attack the Croatian coast. From then on the Dubrovnik and Croatian navy were often to fight together in
defence of the Croatian Adriatic coast.

At the same time Dubrovnik sought security on
the landward side. In about 879 all the Dalmatian
towns paid tribute to Croatian rules to be allowed to
freely possess and till the fields outside the town
walls. Dubrovnik too paid tribute to the princes of
Zahumlje and Travunje to possess in peace its
heritage: Župa, Šumet, Rijeka and Zaton.

In the Middle Ages it was the custom for towns
to worship a patron saint. In 972, during a siege of
the Venetians, Dubrovnik chose as its protector St.
Blasius. From then on the cult of that saint became
the symbol of the town's freedom.

In about 999 Dubrovnik became independent in
the ecclesiastical sense. It became an archbishopric
and metropolic whose ecclesiastical power was acknowledged by the neighbouring Slav bishoprics.

In the 11th century stratification of the inner
social structure started: on one side were the nobility
(nobiles), and on the other the common people
(populas, plebs). This social division was to last until
the end of Dubrovnik's independent political life.

The rule of Byzantium never hindered Dubrovnik's economic development. In the 12th century
Dubrovnik signed treaties of friendship, peace and
free trade with many towns: Molfetta, Pisa, Kotor,
Rovinj, Ravenna, Omiš, Fano, Ancona. It obtained
from Byzantium the privilege of free trade in the
whole empire. In 1186 it signed a peace treaty with
Stefan Nemanja, ruler of Raška, and in 1189 with
Kulin Ban of Bosnia. From then on Dubrovnik caravans were to be found throughout the rocky Balkans,
carrying ore, slaves, animals and farm and rural
products, etc.

Venice, which was to became and remain Dubrovnik's century-long rival, started to hinder its
successful economic start. During the Crusades
from the end of the 11th to the second half of the
13th century Venice, together with Pisa and Genoa,
became master of all the more important trading
posts of the Adriatic, Ionian and Aegean Seas and
the Levant. It became a world power, the strongest
merchant force of the Mediterranean. For Venice the
way to success, security and greatness led through
the Adriatic. If it did not firmly rule and control all the
strategic ports and islands of the eastern Adriatic, its
world dominance would not be assured. Thus in
1202 Venice conquered Zadar with the help of the
Crusaders and in 1205 Dubrovnik also acknowledged its supreme rule, and was to remain under
Venetian sovereignty until 1358.

Venice considered Dubrovnik a dangerous rival
and tried to deflect the town's trading interests inland
to the Balkan hinterland. To stimulate such trade it
granted various privileges. At the same time it
hindered and thwarted maritime trade. As a result of
this policy the inhabitants of Dubrovnik three times
rebelled against Venetian presence in their town and
tried to get Venice off their backs. But during the
13th century they had no success.

Even under these conditions Dubrovnik developed and extended its land and trading connections. Although special contacts with the ports of central and southern Italy and with Croatian and Dalmatian towns were made, profitable markets from the Black Sea to Gibraltar were not neglected.

In 1272 Dubrovnik voted and confirmed its civic Statues - its basic laws. In it are codified the legal norms of the internal and external political life of the commune, administration, inheritance law, maritime affairs, town planning, etc. Then came 1277 and the Customs Law, which determined the duty for imported and exported goods. From 1278 onwards archives have been preserved, which were kept methodically until the fall of the Republic. They contain data not only about all the forms and branches of everyday, political, diplomatic, maritime, mercantile etc. life of old Dubrovnik, but also about its hinterland, and the towns of the Adriatic and Mediterranean seas. In that century the town was surrounded by walls and got its basic present shape.

In the 14th century the main monasteries were built, the Franciscan and Dominican, also the church of St. Blasius, and a new Cathedral was built on the foundations of the original 7th-8th century Cathedral (according to tradition, the King of England Richard the Lion- Hearted founded it in 1192 during his return from the Third Crusade). In the 14th century the pharmacy was founded (1317), the oldest in Europe to work continuously, also the hospital *(Domus Christi)* and the mint; quarantine was established and lazarets founded, the first on the eastern Adriatic coast. Wooden houses were knocked down and stone ones built instead, and the town got its white appearance.

The King of Hungary and Croatia Ludovik I crushed the supremacy of Venice in the Adriatic. By the 1358 Zadar Peace the »Lion of St. Mark« was temporarily forced to leave the eastern Adriatic coast and all its possessions from »the middle of the Kvarner Bay to the boundaries of Durres«. At that time Dubrovnik, which had been part of the Kingdom of Dalmatia and Croatia, became part of the Croato-Hungarian state, and acknowledged the Croato-Hungarian king as its sovereign. From then until 1526, during the whole period through which the Croato-Hungarian protectorate lasted, Dubrovnik was at its peak (from 1526 to 1808 Dubrovnik acknovledged the sovereignty of the Turks). As a Croato-Hungarian protectorate it became a free city-state, which developed into a Republic at the beginning of the 15th century.

Liberty was the main basis for the survival and progress of Dubrovnik, and for this reason the Dubrovnik citizens guarded their liberty jealously, fought for it bravely, put everything else second to it. On Fort Lovrijenac they carved the inscription *Non bene pro toto libertas venditur auro* (Liberty is not sold even for all the gold). They embroidered *Libertas* on flags, flew it on the masts of their ships, carved it on their money, wrote it on all state documents and acts, clothed it inverse, permeated all their aspirations and desires with it. In the community everything was to serve the general good of the state. Above the door to the Grand Council stood the inscription *Obliti privatorum publica curate* (Forget private matters, care for the general good).

When Dubrovnik became part of the Croato-Hungarian community, it was freed from the obstacles and limitations in trade that Venice had imposed in past centuries.

Now its geographically favourable position, open to the wide seas, came fully to expression. Dubrovnik ships cruised the far off seas, anchored in rich ports. Its sailors and merchants sailed the Black Sea to the Crimea and Trapezunt. They were a familiar sight in Constantinople and the Sea of Marmara. Across the islands and ports of the Aegean they traded to Crete, Negroponte, Khios, Fokei, Lesbos, Rhodes. They berthed in the ports of the Levant, in Miletus and Ephesus. They went to Alexandria and the coasts of North Africa. They stopped at the Peloponnese and the coasts of Albania, not to mention the ports of both the coasts of the Adriatic sea. Even before the 14th century Dubrovnik sailors had called at many of those ports, but now they did so more systematically.

Overland trade also developed and branched out. In the hinterland of Dubrovnik, Bosnia and

Serbia, silver, lead and other metals were mined, and gold was dredged (there were mines around Kreševo, Fojnica, Olovo, Trepča, Novo Brdo, Kopaonik etc.). The famous caravan routes, the »Dubrovnik« and »Neretva« roads, wound inland.

Dubrovnik merchants traded at the Drijevo (today Gabela) market-place on the river Neretva. There import-export trade of great volume took place. When it became part of the Croato-Hungarian state the new markets of Croatia, Slavonia, today's Vojvodina, and across the Pannonian plain to Budapest, were opened up to Dubrovnik merchants. The radius of its trade widened and becamegreatly enriched.

When the Turks came to the Balkans in the 14th and 15th centuries they did not interrupt the trend of Dubrovnik's overland trade. Dubrovnik merchants were the first Christian merchants to obtain the right to trade with the »infidel« Turks. This was the famous 1443 »Privilege of Navigation to Eastern Lands« (Privilegium navigationis ad partes orientis), which allowed almost only them to trade with the world of Islam. When the Turks finally gained a stronghold in the Balkans and around the Danube in the 15th and 16th centuries, Dubrovnik was the only South Slav land to remain free. After 1481 it paid an annual tribute (the harač) of 12,500 ducats for that freedom. In return its merchants traded freely in the Turkish Empire, in which at that time roads were safe and there was a single customs market.

In the 16th century the Turks rose to the peak of their power during the time of Suleiman the Magnificent (1520-1566), and with the rise of their power Dubrovnik trade in the Balkans strengthened and spread. At the same time Spain became a great power in the western part of the Mediterranean. Thanks to the discoveries of the New World, in the 16th century she became the leading political and economic power of the West. Through state connections she became mistress of Southern Italy and thus the overseas neighbour of Dubrovnik. Dubrovnik had close ties with Spain, which enabled it to develop maritime trade of great style not only in the western part of the Mediterranean, but also beyond it. Through Gibraltar Dubrovnik seafarers sailed to Portugal, England and the Flanders. They crossed the Atlantic, cast anchor in the Indian Ocean. The inhabitants of Dubrovnik had friendly relations with the Pope. They tried to avoid misunderstandings with Venice and overcome friction.

In such happy circumstances Dubrovnik was a world transit trading centre, exporting raw materials and farm products from the Balkans, and importing high quality goods from the West. Its boats transported goods outside the town port. They were included in the general currents of world trade from the Black Sea to London.

At that time Dubrovnik was one of the first maritime states in the world.

Well developed trade demands the organization of consular representatives. In the 16th century Dubrovnik had 50 consulates in the Mediterranean, one of which was in Cadiz (Portugal). Taking into account its small territory, Dubrovnik had relatively more consulates than much larger and stronger maritime states. In the second half of the 16th century more than 180 ships were registered in Dubrovnik, employing about 3,500 crew members.

Dubrovnik managed to become one of the leading maritime forces thanks to skilful seamanship and diplomacy.

It lived on the edge of the great Turkish Empire, from which it made great profits through trade. On the other hand, it maintained friendly relations with Spain and the Pope, who were in the 16th century at the head of the West's struggle to drive the Turks from the Balkans and the Mediterranean. It was necessary to find adequate diplomatic forms to remain on friendly terms with both great power groups.

The best solution was neutrality. In the 16th century conflict between Spain and Turkey Dubrovnik remained neutral. This allowed it to go on trading even when its friends and protectors were at war with each other. At that time, during certain years of the 16th century, Dubrovnik's trade was 6-7 times greater than during peace, and it was at the peak of its economic power in the 16th century. The city was also one of the greatest craft centres on the Croatian coast. The first South Slav cloth manufactory was founded here. The production of salt was well developed, and so were the following crafts: goldsmiths, building, weaving, leatherworks, furriers, blacksmiths, and especially shipbuilding.

However, the 16th century was also the beginning of crisis and decline. In 1571 the fleet of the so-called Second Holy League, led by Spain, vanquished the Turkish navy at Lepanto. From then on, and especially after the Turkish defeat at Sisak in 1593, the glow of the Turkish crescent started to fade. With the weakening of Turkey the great Dubrovnik trade on the Balkans also declined.

Dubrovnik ships sailed with the Spanish King Philip II's supposedly »Invincible Armanda«, which was intended to smash English power on the seas. But the English beat the Spanish Armanda (1588) and Spain stepped down from the throne of leading world power. The hopes of Dubrovnik linked to the greatness and dominance of Spain sank together with the »Invincible Armada«.

It was not only the economic decline of Turkey and Spain that caused the beginning of the economic decline of Dubrovnik, but also conditions in general. World trade moved out of the Mediterranean because of the discovery of America. States and towns on the Atlantic coast grew. As their maritime power increased, they irresistibly wrested cargoes and profit from the old Mediterranean ports, among them Dubrovnik. Then English, Dutch and French merchant navies penetrated more and more into the Mediterranean, pushing back the old medieval maritime powers, which could no longer compete with them. These new forces got the privileges and alleviations from Turkey that Dubrovnik had once enjoyed. It no langer held the monopoly of trade in the Turkish Empire.

In the 16th century the »price revolution« shook the world, caused by the great influx of gold and silver from American mines into Europe. The value of money decreased, and prices rose. This also was felt in Dubrovnik. Less and less was invested in shipbuilding, seafaring and production. Overland trade also decreased, because in 1592 Venice opened a trading warehouse in Split. Caravans from the hinterland started to go there, bypassing Dubrovnik. In general, mercantile life and traffic declined in Dubrovnik. Realizing this, the inhabitants of Dubrovnik withdrew from active trading. They invested their money in banks and lived off the interest.

In the social sense Dubrovnik society became divided into two basic classes: the owners of capital and the means of production, and those who had neither.

The rich class was itself sub-divided. The nobles were the richest. They were shopowners, wholesale merchants, bankers, houseowners and almost the only landowners. They provided the chief impulse for economic progress and the life of the Republic to the end of the 16th century.

Some of the townsmen *(cives)* were as rich as the nobles: powerful merchants, seamen, members of the brotherhoods of Anthony (founded in 1348) and Lazarus (after 1531). After them came the commoners *(populus),* the middle and small merchants, craftsmen, seafarers and persons of all other middle-class occupations. Townsmen and commoners made as much as they could. An example is the case of Miho Pracat (1527 - 1607), seafarer, who left a great fortune to his town. The clergy - besides owning some land - was weak in the economic sense. The archbishop, head of the church, did not interfere in external politics. Although the citizens of old Dubrovnik were religious, the relationship between the church and state was precisely determined and divided. The oldest and most numerous church order were the Benedictines, who came in the 11th century, followed by the Dominicans and Franciscans in the 13th, and the Jesuits in the 16th century.

The largest womens' order were the Clarissa Nuns, who accepted within the walls of their convent noblewomen only. Many of Dubrovnik's monks were writers, scholars and scientists.

Most numerous among those who had neither capital nor the means of production were the peasants. As a rule they had no land of their own, but tilled the land of the nobles, townspeople and church paying them in kind, although there were cases of payment in money, and some peasants were the landowners' serfs. All of them were personally free, could leave the land whenever they liked, become craftsmen, traders, sailors, or take up any other kind of middleclass occupation.

Until the 14th century much of the work, especially in houses, was done by slaves. In the 15th century the government abolished the slave trade, but slaves could for a time still be obtained for personal use.

There were also workers and seasonal workers in Dubrovnik, day-labourers and other types of occupations needed in a port and mercantile town.

Government was in the hands of the nobles. In the 16th century they formed a closed group. Townsmen and commoners, regardless of wealth, were not allowed to take part in government. All the functions in state government, diplomacy, judicature and finances were held only and exclusively by those of noble birth.

The state was formally represented by the Rector, whose office lasted for a month. The highest legislative body, the greatest power and the bearer of state sovereignty was the Grand Counci (*Consilium majus*), composed of all noblemen over 18 years of age. The Small Council (*Consilium minus*), composed of 11 members elected for a year, was the executive power. The true cabinet was the Senate (*Consilium rogatorum*). It directed external and internal policy, and was composed of 45 members elected for one year.

In these bodies were tempered all the wisdom of government, diplomatic skill and adroitness during all the centuries long ups and downs of the Republic and its ruling class. Except for those councils there were other administrative, judicial etc. bodies.

In the 17th century trade continued to decrease. Then, in 1667, came the terrible blow of the earthquake that speeded Dubrovnik's decline. The town was destroyed, a great part of it burned down, most of the population perished. Although this was a great disaster, its ships in foreign ports remained, its external trade and money in foreign banks. Thanks to that, and to organized help to Dubrovnik from abroad - outstanding in this was Stjepan Gradić in Rome - the town rose from its ruins and ashes, and shone again in its stone glory. It successfully resisted the Turks, who wanted to take it while it still burnt and was defenceless. In his fight to save his homeland the ambassador to the Sultan, Nikolica Bunić, laid down his life in a prison of far away Silistra.

In the 17th century the flag of the West fluttered victoriously, liberating central and eastern Europe from the Turks. In 1684 Dubrovnik renewed the 1358 treaty and acknowledged the sovereignty of the Austrian Emperor, as Croato-Hungarian ruler, but also continued under the submission of the Sultan.

Since then Dubrovnik enjoyed double protection, as it formally owed allegiance to two sovereigns: the Austrian and the Turkish.

In the 18th century Dubrovnik managed to stop the decline of its trade. Magnificent baroque buildings were erected: the Cathedral, the church of St. Blasius, the Jesuit church. Traffic in the port increased. In about 1800 Dubrovnik had consular representatives in over 800 towns and ports. But this was its last rise.

On May 27, 1806, to the notes of the *Marseillaise,* Dubrovnik opened its gates to the French, and on January 31, 1808 the Dubrovnik Republic disappeared forever and the doors closed on its history.

In 1814 French rule was replaced by Austrian, which continued until 1918. Under these new conditions Dubrovnik went on developing like all the other towns in Dalmatia, which was a poor and peripheral part of the Austrian Empire.

Dubrovnik's seafaring, which used to be the main factor of its wealth, declined because it used sailing ships. The first steamship was not bought until 1880. After that came a turning-point in that branch of the economy.

In political life Dubrovnik saw that its progress lay in establishing links with its wider ethnic surroundings. In the revolutionary and tempestous years of 1848 - 1849 it was one of the most ardent supporters of Dubrovnik and the whole of Dalmatia uniting with Croatia. During the 1862 National Revival in Dalmatia Dubrovnik politicians, together with other politicians of the National Party, demanded unity with Croatia and the introduction of the Croatian national language into public life. At that time Dubrovnik gave many politicians of great calibre: Miho Klaić, leader of the National Party, Niko Pucić, Antun Kaznačić, Đuro Pulić etc. When the community of the South Slavs started being formed during World War I, Frano Supilo of Dubrovnik put forward his proposal, a vision of the South Slavs united into a federation.

After the fall of Austria-Hungary National Councils were formed in Dubrovnik, which cleared the way for the uniting of South Slavs in the Kingdom of Serbs, Croats and Slovenes in 1918, which was in 1929 to call itself the Kingdom of Yugoslavia.

In the new state Dubrovnik took the lead in steam shipping. Over 53% of the whole Yugoslav maritime fleet was in Dubrovnik. Its port of Gruž was one of the first Yugoslav ports in tonnage and number of vessels anchored.

Together with seafaring, tourism had already started developing in Dubrovnik. This was the position at the beginning of World War I.

Dubrovnik is small in size but the strangth of its intelligence and spirit always helped it successfully to resist powerful conquerors, before whom much larger and greater states fell, much stronger and more practiced armies, faster and more aggressive navies, more overwhelming arms. It had its own tradition of how to fight for freedom, and how to preserve it. An aristocratic oligarchy like Dubrovnik does not owe its greatness only to its nobles, but to the whole of its society: citizens, commoners, sailors, merchants, craftsmen, peasants and all those whose sweat, work, discipline and self-sacrifice created its glorious past.

It is the fact that it existed as a truly free state for 13 centuries, which was not achieved by many other states and nations, that makes Dubrovnik special in the history of the Croatian and Slav south.

Josip Lučić

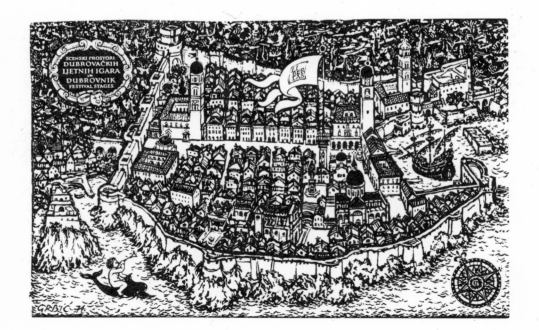

The Maritime Dubrovnik Republic

Seafaring and shipping has been important in Dubrovnik ever since the 9th century, when the town was under the dominance of Byzantium. Dubrovnik ships and sailors joined Byzantine seafarers in various maritime operations. But during the 9th century Byzantine superiority in the Adriatic waned, which made possible a more independent development of life both on and along the whole Adriatic coast. This was a period of conflict between Venice and Croatia for superiority in the Adriatic. In the second half of the 9th century Venetian power decreased, and she paid tribute to the Croats for free navigation in the Adriatic. It was also a period when the maritime economy of the commune of Dubrovnik was well organized, and Dubrovnik became an important trading centre into which led most of the important trading routes from the Balkans. Dubrovnik now flourished for the first time, and its wealth made it interesting for the large and small feudal states in its neighbourhood and hinterland. But not for long. In 1205 Dubrovnik came under the dominance of Venice, and thus remained until 1358. However, seafaring and maritime trade did not decline.

The Seventh Volume of the 1272 Dubrovnik Statutes best illustrates Dubrovnik's very busy maritime life, and the commercial connections it had with many maritime towns.

The Statutes provide various regulations concerning maritime mortgage, harbour taxes, mercantile associations, ships' crews, shipyard workers, the duties and wages of sailors etc. How detailed the Statutes were can best be seen form the fact that even maximum cargoes were stipulated. Ship dimensions are given, and also types of Dubrovnik vessels: *lignum, navigum, navis, galija, navicula, barcusij, kondura etc.*

While Dubrovnik was under the supreme power of Venice its maritime activity was limited, but in 1358 it was liberated from Venice once and for all. Instead of Venetian, Dubrovnik now recognized the supreme power of the Hungaro-Croatian kingdom, and thus obtained greater autonomy. Under new economic and political conditions the maritime and commercial life of all the Croatian coastal communes grew stronger and more advanced. Dubrovnik's merchant marine also developed unhindered. From 1358 to 1420 the Dubrovnik Republic strengthened its position and Dubrovnik became the first and most important port on the eastern Adriatic coast. It had a very developed mercantile fleet. During the 14th century at least two hundred different types of merchant sailing ships were built in Dubrovnik *(koka, kondur, tarid, nav etc.).*

It was not by chance that Dubrovnik paid such attention to its mercantile fleet. It was a transit trading centre for its whole hinterland, and most cirriage was done in Dubrovnik boats. A special place was taken by cargoes of ores coming from Serbia and Bosnia.

In 1526 a new change took place in Dubrovnik's external policy. The Turkish Empire conquered most of the Balkans. Many medieval states, large and small, were destroved or became completely dependent on Turkey. This gave Dubrovnik a special position. It could not resist by arms, but relied on diplomacy. It had no other choice than to pay tribute to the Porte. This was no new solution for Dubrovnik. Even so, the Dubrovnik Republic knew how to preserve the almost complete independence of its policy and state, which was ruled by an oligarchy of Dubrovnik nobles.

Earlier experiences were now applied to new conditions. Thanks to that, and to some other favourable circumstances, the Dubrovnik Republic made use of conditions in general to strengthen its position as a free state, and experienced its greatest economic and cultural rise. The Dubrovnik mercantile fleet was one of the most outstanding in the world. Under the free flag of Dubrovnik seafarers affirmed South Slav seafaring and shipbuilding in the maritime world. Dubrovnik merchant ships sailed between foreign ports, which brought them great profit. At that time Dubrovnik was the most important and strongest Slav maritime commercial centre.

However, the great geographical discoveries in the 16th centry and the opening up of new sea routes resulted in great changes in shipping. The main trade was transferred from the Mediterranean to the Atlantic. Seafaring and shipbuilding developed rapidly on the western coast of Europe, which affected the small Dubrovnik Republic. However, by skillful foreign policy, Dubrovnik managed to take a special place as an economic and maritime power in the eastern Mediterranean. From 1537 to 1540 it was first in maritime trade and shipping in the eastern Mediterranean and in some north African ports. This was the great period of Dubrovnik seafaring, and the city seemed to be one of the world maritime centres. Thanks to developed external policy and international shipping, Dubrovnik shipbuilding was valued very highly. Dubrovnik sailing ships were excellently built and could remain seaworthy for 50 years and longer. The special skill of Dubrovnik shipbuilders was famous in the shipping world, and it was often said of a ship that it was built »in the Dubrovnik manner«. How highly the English regarded the Dubrovnik sailing ships can be seen from the fact that all good and strongly built ships were called »argosy«. The name originated from the Latin name of Dubrovnik - Ragusa. William Shakespeare uses the word argosy, and it rates an entry in the Encyclopedia Britanica. The British have today even given that name to a special BEA aircraft.

From 1570 to 1585 the Dubrovnik Republic had about 200 sailing ships sailing outside the Adriatic, able to carry a total of about 33,000 kara (a kar was a measure for the carrying capacity of a ship, and was rather larger than today's ton). At that time there were about 5,000 seamen in the Republic.

Many of them, and also several members of a same family, gained world fame. The most famous among them was the Ohmučević family; then the Mažibradići, Martolosići, the Olisti-Tasovčići etc. Vice Bune of Lopud was not only an excellent and courageous sailor, he was also a state functionary in the service of Spain. Miho Pracatović-Pracat, also of Lopud, was one of the greatest Dubrovnik seamen.

He was a sailor, then a captain, wholesale merchant, shipowner and banker. In 1638 the Dubrovnik government erected a monument to Pracat, a »worthy citizen«, in the atrium of the Rector's Palace. This was the only monument the patrician government erected to any of its subjects, and thus it paid

respect to this great seaman. Vice Stjepković-Skočibuha from Šipan was also an important personality of maritime Dubrovnik. He was inspired by the spirit and culture of the Renaissance, and left a legacy of fine art monuments in Dubrovnik and Šipan.

Many men of Dubrovnik were outstanding in the nautical sciences, and especially Captain Nikola Sagri-Sagroević, who sailed constantly, until his death in 1573. He was commander of ocean-going ships, and did his writing on board. He published works on nautical sciences.

During the 16th century Dubrovnik seafarers had maritime and trading connections with many lands. They transported goods and passengers between foreign ports and lands, not calling at their home port. They sailed to Albania, Greece, Sicily, the Apennine peninsula, North Africa, Spain, all the way to London.

After the 16th century Dubrovnik naval power decreased. The main cause were external social and economic factors. Already at the end of the 16th and the beginning of the 17th century English, Dutch and other ships came more and more often into the Mediterranean, competing with the merchant fleets of Mediterranean states. Dubrovnik and Venetian ships retreated into the Adriatica and the eastern Mediterranean, which sharpened the rivalry between them. Venice tried not only to destroy Dubrovnik maritime trade, but also to abolish the statehood and legal independence of the Dubrovnik Republic.

In the 17th century the Dubrovnik government instituted many different measures in an attempt to bring the economic life of its state into harmony with new economic conditions. It increased duties, introduced new taxes and passed laws in connection with the fall of the value of silver in Europe. It paid special attention to the increase of production, especially the salts in Ston. It tried to revive the production of cloth, gave special alleviations to shipbuilders, etc.

These new measures contributed to the better organization of Dubrovnik's land trade with the Balkan hinterland, and Dubrovnik, for the last time, became the most important mediator in the exchange of goods between the Turkish Empire and west-European countries. Dubrovnik's landmaritime transit trade with the Balkan lands reached its peak in the middle of the 17th century, yet ten years later it is hardly mentioned.

All the difficulties the Dubrovnik state went through in the 17th century in its struggle for survival and economic progress were increased in 1667, when the town was hit by a catastrophic earthquake, which killed over half of Dubrovnik's inhabitants, did great economic damage and destroyed fine buildings and works of art. There was even a threat that the Dubrovnik Republic would lose its independence. Wishing to renew economic relations severed by the earthquake, and to activate its merchant fleet, Dubrovnik tried to make use of the Venetian-Turkish conflict. But the warring sides started to loot Dubrovnik territory, so that Dubrovnik feared annexation by both. In those most critical moments the Senate sought help from all sides. The most powerful inhabitant of Dubrovnik of that time, Stjepan Gradić, the Pope and diplomatic representatives of European states in Rome all made efforts on behalf of Dubrovnik. The Austrian court also promised help, as it had already started to make far-reching plans in connection with the Balkans. With the help of Madrid and Constantinople Dubrovnik managed to get out of a difficult situation. In the 1669 peace treaty between Venice and Turkey Dubrovnik got a chance to strengthen its international position, to renew the heavily damaged town, and to organize again its maritime trade.

At the end of the 17th century a new power relationship emerged in the Adriatic. Austria established its position, which meant the Dubrovnik government had to reorient its foreign policy. In 1684, through the mediation of Spain, it renewed Austrian protection. At that time its trading connections with Rijeka, Senj, Bakar and other ports of the Croatian coast and Istria grew, and in 1690 the state of Dubrovnik opened a consulate general in Rijeka.

From the 17th century on the best types of sailing ships started being built. At the same time old types were improved and remodelled. A comparison of the Venetian and Mediterranean-French merchant fleets with that of Dubrovnik shows that Dubrovnik shipbuilders concentrated on types of sailing ships that suited them best with regard to conditions in the Mediterranean naval market, and to the navigation qualities of individual types of sailing ships. In the twenties of the 17th century there were the following types of ships in Dubrovnik: *galijun, nava, patač, grip, urka, fregata, fregadun, pinka, pulaka, sajka, tartana, filjuga, marsilijana, berton, šijonica* etc. Most of these were built in the Gruž shipyards, but there were also smaller Dubrovnik shipyards in Brsečine, on Lastovo, Lopud, Šipan, in Slano, Cavtat etc.

In 1599 the total carrying capacity of ships sailing in the Dubrovnik merchant fleet was 23,720 *kara.* From 1597 to 1604 there were about 125 sailing ships built for navigation outside the Adriatic. In 1605 only 68 sailing ships are mentioned, with a total carrying capacity of 17,345 *kara.* The owners of those ships were from Dubrovnik, Zaton, Cavtat, Pelješac, Koločep, Trsteno, Šipan, Slano, Rijeka Dubrovačka, Ston, Broc etc. Over 3,500 men sailed them. In one of the most critical periods in Dubrovnik history (from 1667 to 1695) the merchant fleet of the Dubrovnik Republic had 75 sailing ships, with a carrying capacity of 6,095 *kara.*

The given data show that during the 17th century the Dubrovnik merchant fleet gradually decreased both in number of vessels and in their carrying capacity.

Dubrovnik ships sailed on and outside the Adriatic, chiefly in the central and eastern Mediterranean, and especially on the following lines: Genova-Livorno-Naples-Messina-Palermo-Lagosta-Crete-Alexandria-Izmir-North Africa-Greek archipelago-Constantinople. Sailing ships on coastal lines had maritime-trading connections with almost all the more important ports of the eastern Adriatic coast, and especially with Senj, Bakar, Rijeka, Kotor, Herceg-Novi, Perast, Budva etc. They also called at Albanian ports. During the 17th century many foreign ships, especially French *tartane and pulake,* and many Italian and British sailing ships called in trade in Dubrovnik.

During the whole 17th century the Dubrovnik merchant fleet was internationally active and participated greatly in the transport of goods and cargoes of international trade, so that during some decades of the 17th century the total number of Dubrovnik ships was greater than the number of ships in the Venetian merchant fleet.

Especially important for Dubrovnik's transit trade was the existence of the lazaret. It is a monumental and very functional building, in which large warehouses and spacious rooms for merchants and passengers on longer stay can still be seen. It had special administration, and a permanent guard of paid soldiers. It is an important historical monument that has only recently been completely restored, and is in an excellent state of preservation.

In spite of very well developed and widely acknowledged shipbuilding, Dubrovnik did not have enough experts to build warships. The Dubrovnik state never had a large navy. In the 17th century Dubrovnik had about ten types of warships (*velika galija, fusta, galijica, mala* and *velika fregata, brigantin, ormanica, fuljuga, duga barka* etc.). They were used in the defense of state frontiers and for the protection of marchant ships and their cargoes. They also protected the lives and property of Dubrovnik citizens, especially those on the islands and in coastal regions, which in the 17th century were often prey to looting by pirate ships.

The general 18th century political, economic and social conditions were reflected on life in the Dubrovnik Republic. The worst period for Dubrovnik seafaring and shipping was during the first three decades of the 18th century. In the period from 1744 to 1761 Dubrovnik maritime life flourished.

The largest item in state income were various direct and indirect taxes on the maritime economy. The Dubrovnik government took many measures to strengthen its merchant fleet as much as possible. With that purpose the *Regulations of the Dubrovnik Republic for National Navigation* were passed in 1745. They supplemented already existing legal norms about supervision on ships, crews, etc. In 1751 that maritime edict was extended further, and was printed for the first time in 1784. The second edition appeared in 1794 and had 60 sections. The *Regulations* mention the Dubrovnik maritime body, the »Chief Administration for Seafaring and Navigation«, which treated exclusively maritime problems, superintended navigation, carried out the government's maritime policy, settled maritime lawsuits etc. The *Regulations* also determined the rights and duties of Dubrovnik consuls connected to Dubrovnik ships, and concular taxes paid by boats in foreign ports. They are the concluding phase of the 1,000-year-long efforts of Dubrovnik to organize as best it could its merchant fleet, and maritime life in general. Ships'crews were the most important factor in the development of maritime and economic life in the Dubrovnik Republic.

The *Regulations* determined that the crew of Dubrovnik sailing ships must be composed of Dubrovnik citizens - except for some exceptions. The total number of persons employed on Dubrovnik ships sailing outside the Adriatic in the middle of the 18th century was over 2,200 seamen. There were over 400 shipowners and co-owners. If we add many other occupatios connected to the maritime economy, for instance shipbuilders, fishermen, workers in the salt-flats, longshoremen, consular employees (whose chief duty it was to admit and dispatch Dubrovnik ships in foreign ports) and others employed in seafaring, we get a very large number, in relation to the approximately 25,000 inhabitants of the Dubrovnik Republic. This shows the maritime orientation of the Dubrovnik state.

During the 17th, 18th and 19th centuries many seamen of the eastern Adriatic coast, who were not Dubrovnik citizens, sailed on Dubrovnik ships. The cooperation between Dubrovnik citizens and inhabitants of the coastal regions of Brač, Boka Kotorska, Hvar, Korčula, Makarska, Premud, Split, Trogir, Vis, Zadar, the whole of Dalmatia, the Croatian Primorje and Istra, was many-sided. During the centuries a great number of inhabitants of what is today Yugoslavia constantly took part in Dubrovnik maritime life (regardless of the state frontiers of those days, which separated them from each other) very successfully. This is another fact which affirms that the process of creating a common life for all the Yugoslav peoples has a long history.

Some seamen stood out in scholarly, cultural and scientific ability. Ivan A. Kaznačić (1758-1850) was an ocean-going captain, chart-maker, diplomat and writer. He was first schooled in the Collegium Ragusinum, then became a watch-maker, and then took up navigation. When he was twenty he became a captain. In 1798 he stopped sailing and turned to sea trading, also becoming director of the largest Dubrovnik maritime insurance company. He also drew sea charts.

Seeing the great ability and culture of that experienced practical man, excellent maritime theoretician, chart-maker and writer, in 1803 the Dubrovnik government named Captain Kaznačić its consul-general in Genova. Even earlier, and especially in the 18th centuries, the Dubrovnik government named many Dubrovnik captains its consular representatives in foreign ports.

Among the seamen and merchants who were not Dubrovnik citizens, but who moved there permanently, a special place is certainly taken by the shipowner, merchant and captain Jakov Priskić from Lovran. Making use of his experiences of thirty years he spent in Dubrovnik, Captain Priskić organized far-reaching trade between Balkan lands under Austrian dominance. Priskić's trade connections extended from Albania, Serbia, Macedonia, Bulgaria, through Bosnia, Montenegro and Herzegovina, to his permanent business headquarters in Dubrovnik, on to Senj, Bakar, Rijeka, Lovran, Rovinj, Trieste, Ljubljana and Slovenia, and further into the interior of northern Croatia, even reaching Austria.

The renewal of the Dubrovnik merchant fleet and the great revival of maritime trading increased the number of Dubrovnik consulates. In the second half of the 18th and the beginning of the 19th century the Dubrovnik Republic had consular representatives in over eighty places, including: Lisbon, Madrid, Gibraltar, Malaga, Tangier, Carthage, Barcelona, Marseil-

les, Nice, Majorca, Tunis, Tripoli, Genova, Livorno, Venice, Pesaro, Ancona, Naples, Palermo, Malta, Algiers, Brindisi, Taranto, Trieste, Rijeka, Skadar, Dürres, Valona, Corfu, Salonika, Varna, Izmir, Constantonople, Latakia, Rhodes, Alexandria etc. This truly great number of consular representatives best shows how the Dubrovnik marchant fleet flourished. Their position shows some of the important routes taken by Dubrovnik martime trade in the 18th and the beginning of the 19th century. Dubrovnik ships sailed most between Levantine ports and west-European lands, through the whole Mediterranean, the Black Sea and the Adriatic. From Livorno, Marseilles, Naples, Izmir and several Spanish ports Dubrovnik ships carried cargo to Baltimore, New York, Philadelphia, Boston, Havana, Cap France, Martinique, St. Bartolomy, St. Thomas, San Domingo, Brazilian ports etc. Maritime commercial connections of Dubrovnik with North, Central and South America took place according to momentary conditions on the world maritime market.

At that time Dubrovnik ships were third in the world (not counting Britain) in average mean size. In total size of ships they were twelfth (in front of the Papal State, Piemont, Toscana, Rostock, Danzig, Russia, Prussia and Venice without Boka Kotorska).

From 1787 to 1793 Dubrovnik had about 190 long distance ships with a total carrying capacity of about 15,000 *kara*. At the same time Stockholm had a total of 259 shipa (including the smallest) with 48,574 tons carrying capacity, and Göteborg a total number of about 200 boats of all categories carrying 29,970 tons. In 1805 the total number of ships sailing outside the Adriatic was 280 sailing ships of international importance with over 25,000 *kara* carrying capacity. At that time there were seven thousand seamen, shipbuilders, fishermen, shipowners and co-owners and other naval experts in the Dubrovnik state. That number proves most strongly what maritime economy meant for the Dubrovnik Republic, which at that time had about 35,000 inhabitants. The size and importance of the Dubrovnik long-distance merchant fleet (not to mention the much greater number of smaller vessels, which sailed in the Adriatic and locally), which bore the white flag of St. Blasius or that with the inscription *Libertas* on all seas, and the role that fleet played in the economic and social development of Dubrovnik and its close and more distant hinterland, can only be seen if it is compared with the Venetian mercantile marine sailing under the flag of the winged lion of St. Mark with a sword in his hand (here are included the ships of Boka Kotorska and other regions of what is today Yugoslavia). At the beginning of the 18th century the Venetian merchant fleet had 60 ships sailing outside the Adriatic, and by 1779 that number increased to 392. However, it must be stressed that smaller ships were included here. In that period Venetian shipowners bought and built ships outside Venice also, among other places in Dubrovnik.

At that time Dubrovnik very successfully made use of the great boom in seafaring, leasing space on ships for the transport of various goods, so that it was famous in the whole seafaring world. Dubrovnik sailors were very highly esteemed even in Venice, and during some decades of the 18th century Dubrovnik sailing ships maintained the most important Venetian commercial connections with ports of the western Mediterranean, and even Atlantic ports.

Dubrovnik crews were better paid than Venetian crews, which can be seen from the fact that about 1,400 foreign sailors were employed on Dubrovnik sailing ships, and only a very small number (about ten!) Dubrovnik sailors sailed on foreign boats.

Between 1797 and 1806 the merchant fleet of this small free maritime state was the most successful and best organized Mediterranean merchant fleet sailing under a neutral flag. This was in fact the swan song of a millenium-long well developed and organized maritime life, which is part of the history of world maritime trade and shipping.

In 1808 the thousand-year-long thread of Dubrovnik maritime life was broken off and the importance of Dubrovnik, as a world maritime-mercantile state, destroyed.

The industrial revolution shook the foundations of maritime economy, and in the 19th century seafering and shipping went through changes that could earlier not have been dreamed of. Steam overpowered sail. On the eastern Adriatic coast those events came very late because of Austria's economic policy. It was not until 1880 that Dubrovnik obtained its first steam ship to sail on a local line. This was the beginning of a new area in Dubrovnik seafering and steam shipping, in which Dubrovnik was later to take again one of the first and leading places on the Yugoslav coast.

The openning of a permanent state nautical school in 1852; the laying of the Sarajevo-Dubrovnik railway line; the building of Gruž into the mercantile port of modern Dubrovnik; the beginning of the steam-ship era, together with the final strong development and rapid decline of the Pelješac sails - all those mark the most important moments in the maritime history of Dubrovnik at the end of the 19th century.

In 1910 Austria-Hungary had 365 steam ships with 777,729 tons carrying capacity. Dubrovnik had 37 steam ships with 66,853 tons carrying capacity. In 1939 Yugoslavia had 177 steam ships with 394,518 tons carrying capacity, and of that Dubrovnik had 48 steam ships with 167,194 tons carrying capacity.

A very small part of Dubrovnik's maritime history is told in museum language by exhibits in the Maritime Museum of the Yugoslav Academy of Sciences and Arts in Dubrovnik, which is situated in the harbour fort of Sveti Ivan.

Josip Luetić

Architecture and Sculpture

The time when the settlement and later the town and the centre of the small South Slav state of Dubrovnik was founded is still open to discussion. There have been settlements here for over a thousand years. Legend says that refugees from nearby Epidaurum built a town on a rock that jutted out of the sea and was separated from the shore by a narrow channel. Thus the first name of the settlement was Lausa, which means rock in ancient Greek. Most recent research, however, shows that at the time when Epidaurum was destroyed a settlement, if not a town, must already have existed here, which could have taken in the refugees from devastated Epidaurum.

Regardless of the exact time when the town was founded, during its whole existence its inhabitants showed and proved that they knew how to build a town, and not one only. In architecture, as in other activities, some of their buildings, fortifications and ports, churches and monasteries, houses and mansions, showed a feeling for proportion and the knowledge of how to solve even the most complicated problems often imposed on them by the constricted and not very happily chosen site. That site was excellent only for defense, but not for the normal development of a large settlement. They managed to solve not only the urbanistic problems of the town of Dubrovnik, but also of the small towns of Ston, Ston Mali, Cavtat and Molunat. Later they included individual buildings with a great feeling for measure, always in human scale.

As in the whole of Europe, here also civilizations and cultures succeeded one another and left traces, especially in architecture. Here too, as in the rest of Europe, towns, homes, mercantile, harbour and other buildings were built and planned, also churches, monasteries, buildings of recluse etc.

From the earliest periods of the present era it is the remains of churches that have chiefly been preserved, especially in the wider Dubrovnik region. It is certain that Early Christian churches also existed on the site of the oldest part of the town of Dubrovnik, but except for some fragments of decorative sculpture from the 5th and 6th centuries, no building has as yet been located.

In the beginning the traditions of Roman, and then Byzantine architecture were continued. Later, from the 9th to the 12th century, a special type of architecture evolved. That of the pre-Romanesque period, it had its prototypes, but is so typical for southern Dalmatia that it is necessary to give it special mention. The octafoil building with a round base, in the small village of Ošlje in the Dubrovnik coastal region, dates from the 8th century. Its walls, still in quite a good state of preservation, and its newly discovered narthex, indicate a type of building known in Dalmatia, but its proportions make it one of the most beautiful specimens of the type. Other buildings of this pre-Romanesque period are scattered around the whole Dubrovnik region. Many are in ruins, but some have been preserved, especially on the Elaphite islands (Koločep, Lopud, Šipan), but also on Mljet, the Pelješac peninsula, in Ston, Konavli and elsewhere.

These buildings have small dimensions, and a typical base: a parallelogram with an apse square from the outside, and semicircular or square from the inside, which continues into a semi-dome. Typical is a small dome in the middle of the nave, whose outside shape is square and has a hipped roof. The outside, and especially the inside treatment of the walls of these buildings are well developed, so that buttresses, blind arcades, small consoles etc. are often found. The whole interiors of those churches, including the ceilings, were originally decorated with frescoes, and very often the outside walls also.

In most of them the frescoes have been destroyed or are in a very bad condition, so that today very few remain. Best preserved are the frescoes in the pre-Romanesque church of St. Michael *(sv. Mihajlo)* in Ston.

The most important characteristic of this period and this architecture is interlaced ornamentation, decorative plasterwork that frames doors, windows and stone church furniture with geometrical ornaments, most often in plaits. In the town of Dubrovnik the following churches from that period have been preserved: St Nicholas *(sv. Nikola)* in Prijeko (11th century), the church of the Transfiguration *(Sigurata,* 11th century). Less well preserved are the remains of the first Dubrovnik Cathedral of St. Peter the Great, with a crypt that can be dated between the 9th and the 10th century.

Pre-Romanesque architecture in the building of churches dated from the 9th to the 12th century. This was a period during which Dubrovnik developed into a more coherent community, not only as a town, but also as a commune, and the contours of the future small state could already be seen. Thus it is not surprising that its first cathedral bears all the marks of that architecture. Although still insufficiently explored, research carried out to date establishes that the first Dubrovnik cathedral was a vaulted building with a dome and a crypt. There is a short description of it by a contemporary who saw it in 1440, Filip de Diversis. This famous building was almost completely destroyed in the Great Earthquake in 1667.

In 949, in his work *De administrando imperio* the Byzantine Emperor Constantine Porphyrogenitus said that Dubrovnik had a very fine church dedicated to St. Stephen. It is in the ruins of a later Gothic church, which was also called St. Stephen *(sv. Stjepan).*

Right by the old town core there are more remains of churches from that period (St. Andrew, St. Luke *(sv. Andrija, sv. Luka).*

It is a historical fact that there was already a settlement here before the 7th century, which provided hospitality and a roof over the heads for the citizens of devastated Epidaurum. The appearance of this settlement, or town, is unknown, because today's town was built on its remains. Strong earthquakes also changed the appearance and face of that old settlement, so that finally, all that has been found is some 5th and 6th century decorative plasterwork. The size of the oldest nucleus can be discerned to a certain extent. It was much smaller than today's town, and was situated on the highest part of the rocky islet of Lava, in the part of the town today called Kaštio. It is assumed that in the 5th century there was a settlement there. It might have been enlarged for the first time when the inhabitants of Epidaurum fled from their destroyed and looted town and settled here, where they felt to a certain extant safe and defended.

The Dubrovnik Statues *Liber statorum civitatis Ragusii* date from 1272, which means that the habitual earlier written and unwritten laws were then legalized. The Fifth Volume of the Statues describes the building of the town, so that these Stautes also legalize the exsiting conditions in the part of the town already built. Thus the 1272 Statutes teach us something about the earlier spatial appearance of the town. They show that the highest point of the islet of Lava was called Kaštio *(castellum).* They also show that the old town walls still existed at the foot of the islet to the north and to the east. Chroniclers say that those walls were built of lime and stone at the end of the 8th century. Today's Karmen quarter, to the east of the oldest town core, was a suburb. When it also was encircled by walls and became part of the town, its name of Pustijerna remained, which originates from the words *post terra* (outside the town). The town developed outside the walls also, on the sites of today's Gundulićeva poljana and the Rector's Palace. There was a suburban settlement of wooden houses there.

During the 10th and 11th centuries the small sea channel that separated the islet of Lava from the shore was filled in. The Slavs had already settled on the shore. In the 11th and at the beginning of the 12th century the whole space that is today fortified started to be surrounded by walls, except for the site of the Dominican Monastery, which became part of the town somewhat later.

The building of those new walls, which are thought originally to have been dry-stone, wood and earth, lasted for rather a long time.

The 1272 Statutes mention them as still being built, while annexes from 1296 mention them as finished. It is understandable that this refers to walls built from lime and stone.

In the middle of August 1296, there was a great fire in Dubrovnik, which changed the appearance of the town to a certain extnet. About thirty days later important regulations were passed about new building in the town, which referred to the building of the quarter called Prijeki. For the southern part of the new town, from Placa to the walls of the old town, regulations were implemented, and several new streets were laid. 1296 regulations regulated the final ground plan of Dubrovnik, which has remained the same until today. Some small changes took place during the building of the Rupa Building, when ruins from today's Gundulićeva poljana were removed after the Great Earthquake in 1667 and its surroundings changed, and when the Sponza Manison and the Jesuit Collegium were built.

In 1310 the Dominican Monastery was also surrounded by the town walls, so that this large complex of buildings became part of the town.

In 1315 a plan for building the entire Prijeki quarter was made, which included the whole area north of the main town street Placa. By order of the government the Franciscan Monastery, which had until then been a bit further than Pile, moved there.

This ended the spatial planning of the town of Dubrovnik, and it has remained thus until today. Some small, but not essential changes and rebuilding took place over the centuries, especially after the Great Earthquake in 1667. April 6, 1667, was one of the most tragic days of Dubrovnik. The earthquake that shook the town and its neighborhood in the early morning hours destroyed it almost completely. What was not destroyed by the earthquake was burned in the fire, which was said to have lasted for three days. Thanks to great sacrifices made by the inhabitants of this smail republic and to their inexhaustible vitality, the town was rebuilt very quickly. Luckily, its walls had withstood the earthquake, but almost all the dwelling-houses and many public and ecclesiastical buildings were totally destroyed. The Dubrovnik Cathedral, to whose building the King of England Richard the Lion Hearted had contributed, was completely destroyed. The large church of the Franciscan Monastery burned down, the first Dubrovnik Cathe-dral of St. Peter was destroyed, the Rector's Palace was badly damaged, and also the large fountain by Onofrio de la Cava. The monasteries of St. Thomas, St. Šimun, St. Andrew and others were erased from the face of the earth, never to be renewed.

After the great earthquake some smaller spatial adjustments were made. The houses and streets of today's Gundulićeva poljana were never rebuilt. A large square was made there, which passes into a large baroque stairway on the south. This is the only Dubrovnik area concieved in a baroque manner, and at the top was built the large baroque Jesuit Church.

Except for the already mentioned small changes, today's appearance of the town is identical to that of the 14th century. the facades of the houses changed because of the earthquake, and were replaced by baroque facades, but their ground plans remained intact.

The main characteristic, and thus also the great value of Dubrovnik, is that it was, for the most part, built according to plan. A sense for simplicity and entirety gave it a special beauty and harmony. There is no obtrusiveness nor exaggerated luxury, everything breathes of architectural purity. Houses and monasteries, churches and fountains, small and simple mansions and more luxurious ones are all included and mingle with such harmony, that they enoble and enhance each other's value.

Dubrovnik cannot be described without the qualities of its strictly planned area being stressed. Its inhabitants knew how to build on a constricted space, limited by monumental walls, with restrained architectural genius, and at the same time to make subject everything to man. The streets are distributed with great feeling for measure, man feels himself to be at the centre, everything is subjected to him, and human beings are not dwarfed by space and height.

The inhabitants of Dubrovnik built their town with a wise rationality. They managed to give it the stamp of their own originality. Dubrovnik has no ideal, it is its own - original.

The Dubrovchani surrounded their master-piece, their town, with great and monumental walls. These walls, which had earlier been built in a more modest and simple technique, were built to defend the town and the people from enemies, to defend their so much loved liberty. And they loved their liberty above everything, and subjected everything to it.

The building, additions and rebuilding of today's walls lasted from the 13th century. They were built and added to according to the armament of the time. In the 15th century outer walls were built, towers raised and those parts that were most imperilled strengthened.

In full length the walls are 1,940 metres. They are up to 25 metres high, and have three round and 12 square towers, 2 corner fortifications, 5 bastions and one large fortress. The walls are 4 to 6 metres thick on the land side, and 1 to 3 metres thick facing the sea. As arms were modernized, so the walls were strengthened and added to. To protect the towers and fortifications on the land side, especially to the west and north, in the 15th century outer walls with scarps were constructed. They started from the only casemate tower of Bokar, and have one large and 9 smaller semicircular bastions. The walls with towers and bastions are especially impressive. They were not only monumental and of great use, but also give a special beauty to the play of light and shadow.

The town has four entrance gates, two to the land and two to the sea. The land gates face the east and west, while both the sea gates face the town harbour. Stone bridges connected the land town gates to wooden drawbridges, for better defense.

To the east and west of the town there are two independent fortresses, Revelin and Lovrijenac. It is not known precisely when Lovrijenac was built. It is first mentioned in writing in 1301, but by then it was already built. Revelin was built in the 16th century, when the town and state were again endangered at the time of the First Holy League.

Impressive Lovrijenac not only dominates the town, but is a stroke of architectural genius. It is a free-standing fortress that gives the impression of a stone ship proudly resisting anyone who so much as dares to approach Dubrovnik. This fortress is separated from the town, and the master of Lovrijenac could possibly become the master of the town. That is why the wise warning. *NON BENE PRO TOTO LIBERTAS VENDITUR AURO* (Do not sell liberty for all the gold in the world) stands above the entrance to this magnificent fortress.

Revelin stands on the opposite side of the town and defends its eastern entrance. A ditch, which surrounded most of the town, again for better defense, separates them. The name Revelin itself is a fortificational term used for fortifications that defend the weakest parts of a town. The first Revelin was started in 1463 on the present site. It was a fortification of much smaller dimensions. In 1538 the Dubrovnik Senate accepted the plan for the present Revelin by Antun Ferramoldino. This massive fortress was built in a hurry, chiefly because of danger from Venice. Simple in proportions, but massive and threatening, it defends the town's most vulnerable point - the entrance from the not-so-well defended eastern side.

In 1482 the building and strengthening of the town port was finished. Pasko Miličević, the unusually versatile engineer, who worked for a long time, also made the project for this great work. It is still in its original form, but after the fall of the Dubrovnik Republic two small towers, the Rector's and Peskarija, were removed, and also the battlements and part of the tower of Sveti Luka. The harbour was defended from the sea by the fort of Sveti Ivan and the large break-water Kaše. An enormous iron chain between the break-water and the fort used to stop enemy ships from stealing into the port and town.

At the bottom of the town port was the large Arsenal, with four large arches, for the storage and building of boats. The building of the Arsenal is already mentioned in the 1272 Statutes. Most of Dubrovnik's wealth was made on the sea. How important the inhabitants of Dubrovnik considered ships can be seen from the fact that they built the Arsenal almost in the middle of the town. Another smaller arsenal, for smaller boats, was built in 1412

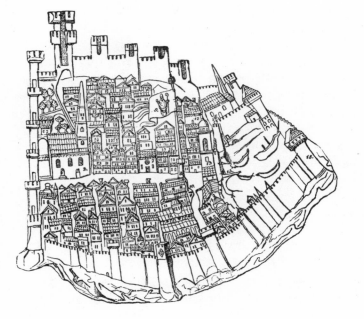

and also situated in the town port, but during Austro-Hungarian occupancy it, and the towers already mentioned, were knocked down and the harbourmaster's office built on the foundations.

The names of the many masters and builders who built the walls are not known, especially those of earlier periods. In the 15th and 16th centuries names of both local and foreign masters are found. The Dubrovnik Historical Archives are an inexhaustible source for the history of Dubrovnik architecture. Thus they show that the Pile Gate in the west was planned and built in 1462 by the Tuscan architect Michelozzo di Bartolomeo, who also built Minčeta Tower, but did not finish it. This magnificent tower, which dominates the town, was finished by Juraj Dalmatinac in the second half of the 15th century.

The following local masters took part in the building of the town walls and fortifications: Nićifor Ranjina and Miho Hranjac, Mato Martini, Marin Držić etc. The monument to all those known and unknown builders of the Dubrovnik town walls is their work, the pride of past, present and future generations.

The massive Dubrovnik town walls, which guarded the property and liberty of the town, are the finest monument to the sacrifices and efforts of Dubrovnik inhabitants of old. All the citizens of this town equally endured great privations, so that their safety, their lives and their possessions would be guarded and preserved as best they could in those difficult and dangerous days which devastated Europe. The original beauty and state of preservation of the Dubrovnik town fortifications, which were not even changed by catastrophic earthquakes, and the originality of the old town core, prove that those who built them had an especially strong feeling for order, functionality and utility, and also for all that is beautiful, noble and harmonious.

The regular grid-like distribution of town streets, confident urbanistic solutions without exaggeration and megalomania, restraint and economy, simplicity and measure, are the characteristics of Dubrovnik urbanism. Such a feeling for measure could have been born and preserved only in a strong and mature community. The main strength and basic quality of the town is characterized by this sense of urbanistic maturity, where general harmony comes first, and is then enriched detail. The urbanistic expressions are convincing and stately, and show a good feeling for proportion and monumentality. But in that monumentality there is nothing insulting and no overbearing propaganda. The Palace, mansions, churches and monasteries are knowingly situated on dominant and important sites, but built in measured architecture, without any wish to stand out at the expense of what is near them.

Thus building their town, the Dubrovchani placed the seat of their government - the Rector's Palace, state buildings and two important ecclesiastical building, the Cathedral, the seat of ecclesiatstical power, and the church of the town patron St. Blasius, in the eastern part of the town, behind the town port. These buildings form a square. Here the official life of the town and the state took place.

Down the main town street Placa were shops and workshops belonging to craftsmen and merchants. business life hummed in this magnificent street, which is in fact a great hall whose ceiling is the sky, blue or scattered with southern stars. Several more streets were used for merchants and craftsmen. The others were chiefly for living in. Because of constricted space, any that was available had to be used as rationally as possible.

Dwelling-houses and other Romanesque buildings of the old town have almost completely disappeared. In that period wooden houses were still built, but in time stone ones took their place.

One of the reasons for this are government decisions prohibiting building in wood, especially after the great fire in 1296. Some remains of Romanesque architecture are left, but only fragmentarily. Several catastrophes, earthquakes and fires, ravaged Dubrovnik and carried away both modest Romanesque buildings, and the richest mansions and churches.

Everything seems to indicate that the Gothic style came to Dubrovnik very early. The town gates by the fish market are already mentioned in the 1272 Statutes. These gates are Gothic, and so is the statue of St. Blasius above them.

The size of the stone rectangles and the Gothic arch of the portal bespeak early Dubrovnik Gothic art. The inhabitants of Dubrovnik grew to love the style and built in it for a long time. It is supposed that at the time of its greatest flourishing in the 15th and 16th centuries Dubrovnik was a predominantly Gothic city.

Renaissance was brought to Dubrovnik by the Tuscan architect M. Michelozzo di Bartolomeo (1461-1464), but he had a difficult job to supersede the Gothic. Gothic elements can almost always be found on buildings conceived in the Renaissance manner. Thus a curious symbiosis of those styles took place, that is found only in Dubrovnik. It is completely understandable that during additions and renewals these styles could merge, but in Dubrovnik building, both ecclesiastical and profane, they were connected from the outset. It must also be mentioned, however, that quite a large number of Renaissance buildings with no Gothic additions have also been preserved.

The baroque style came to Dubrovnik after the earthquake. This was a time when foreign architects were invited, like Mario Gropelli from Venice, to build and renew the church of St. Blasius and the admiralty. A second-rate architect, with no inventivity or spirit, he could not create anything that would serve as a lasting mark of the time. The same happened with the building of the Cathedral on the site of the ruined old Romanesque one.

To make life as good and comfortable as possible, each dwelling-house was high with rather a small ground-plan. Thus one family had a ground floor, upper floors and a loft in which, because of the possibility of fire, and also because it was sunny, there was the kitchen and a kind of living-room. Thus the same house had both shade and sun. In the summer the lower, cooler rooms could be used, and in the winter the sunny warm lofts.

The facade of dwelling-houses were always simple. The doors and windows were always in proportion with the walls. Their frames were fine but of simple profile, stylistically corresponding to the period they were built in. At each side of the bottom of every window there is a stone console on which a board wasplaced for drying fruit or for flowers. On the upper part of the windows there is a console in the middle, with a circular hole in it, called an »ear«, Through the hole a wooden shaft was placed from which hung a piece of cloth to protect the interior of the house from the looks of others, and also to protect it from the sun and heat. According to the wealth of their owner, ordinary town houses had richer or more modestly decorated entrance doors. Some also had balconies, but these were only built until the 1667 earthquake, because after that year the building of balconies was prohibited.

The houses and mansions of the nobles and rich citizens stood out because of the elaborate decorative plasterwork of their portals, windows, and even balconies. Lovely Gothic triforia and quadriforia could be seen, intricate carving, lacelike balcony balustrades. Unfortunately, very few of those luxurious facades were preserved, and the ardourous economic conditions of the almost completely demolished town did not allow them to be renewed in the original state, but only as far as conditions allowed. Several original mansions were preserved, chiefly in the Karmen quarter and Puntijerna, where the effect of the earthquake was somewhat smaller

One of the most beautiful is the Restić Mansion in Pustijerna. Its very decorated late-Gothic facade shows great skill in achieving unobtrusive luxury.

The Renaissance mansion of the citizen family of Skočibuha, in this same part of the town, shows that citizens always built in the newest style. The nobles very often built in late Gothic, seeming to consider the Gothic style the one for the ruling class. Because of cramped space, this several-storey building has facade decoration only on the higher storeys: four large square, and then arched windows framed with pillars and gables.

In the north of the town in Prijeki street were also several lovely, and for Dubrovnik conditions, rich buildings. Outstanding among them is the mansion of the citizen family of Isusović. Gothic-Renaissance in style, part of it was unfortunately knocked down and later badly rebuilt.

Several other mansions show that there was no uniformity of decorative plasterwork, or facades, and that each building was original in itself.

The seat of Dubrovnik government was the Rector's Palace. In it, except for the Rector's private rooms and representative halls for offical receptions and audiences, there were also the halls of the Small Council, the Republic Secretary, notary, land-registry and armed goal.

The oldest chronicles show that there used to be a fortified 12th or 13th century castle (castellum) on the site of today's Rector's Palace. In 1435 the gunpowder kept in the armoury exploded, and damaged it badly. The Napolitan architect Onofrio di Giordano de la Cava, who had been summoned to Dubrovnik in the middle of the first half of the 15th century to make plans for and build the waterworks and bring water to Dubrovnik, was commissioned to build a new Rector's Palace on the foundations of the old castle. The new palace had 4 wings that surrounded an interior courtyard, and corner towers. The two on the western facade flank a porch with an arcade of five columns and two semi-columns, which rises to the height of the first floor. Above the ground floor the Palace had a mezzanine and two floors. The second floor was destroyed at the time of the second gunpowder explosion in 1463.

The south-eastern tower of the Palace held the town clock, and the bell for the Cathedral and various other town and state proclamations. The second gunpowder explosion ruined this tower too, so it was decided to transfer the belltower with the clock to another site. At that time the other corner towers also lost their battlements.

The great Renaissance architect Michelozzo di Bartolomeo of Florence was then in Dubrovnik. He was commissioned to draw up plans for a new Palace. However, the cautious and economical Dubrovchani considered the project too expensive and rejected it. Chiefly with the help of local masters, they patched up and mended what had been destroyed. Until 1469 the Florentine stone-mason Salvi di Michiele worked on the repairs.

The great 1667 earthquake damaged the Palace and shook it badly. Stone-cutting was done by Jeronim Škarpa of Korčula.

Onofrio's Palace was built in the late-Gothic style. It seems that he followed the foundations of the old castle: corner towers flanking a porch through which the Palace is entered indicate this. The western entrance-side is most richly decorated. The porch has an arcade whose columns have luxuriously carved capitals. There is a monumental entrance portal, also decoratively framed, above which is a Renaissance seated statue of St. Blasius. The eight two-light windows framed with leaves and human heads, have as their base a richly decorated cornice. Above them is the final cornice, which was changed during the last century.

The other facades of the Palace are either invisible because of other buildings or walls, or, like for instance the southern one, changed appearance in the 17th century. On the western facade of the Palace many Renaissance details mingle with the Gothic. The courtyard, i.e. the inner atrium, is completsly concieved in the Gothic manner. Although it too was damaged, it has been faithfully restored. Its ground floor has archivolts on three sides, while on the fourth are a small water-fountain and a baroque staircase.

On the southern side of the mezzanine is a small indrawn loggia with arches.

The only monument to a man erected by the Dubrovnik government during the twelve centuries of its existence is the monument to the townsman Miho Pracat, because of his exceptional attachment to the town and state. Not, however, wishing to make him too outstanding, in the first half of the 17th century they placed his bust in the atrium of the Rector's Palace, to thank him in that manner for all the good he had done for his homeland.

On the upper-floor gallery small double columns bear arcades. On that gallery is the Palace chapel, whose doorframes, like the other door frames on the gallery, were made after the earthquake.

Local masters did most of the work on the renewal of the Rector's Palace.

From the Palace the neighbouring building, the Palace of the Grand Council, could be reached. Above its door still stands the inscription OBLITI PRIVATORVM PVBLICA CVRATE (Forget private and attented to public matters). This building burnt down at the beginning of the 19th century, so it was torn down in 1864 and today's commune building built on the foundations. Drawings from the middle of the 19th century show that the old palace had a Gothic three-light window on the first floor, with a single-light window on each side of it, and that it was very similar in appearance to the Sponza Mansion. Thus it can be assumed that it was built by the same architect - the local master Pasko Miličević.

Adjoining the Palace of the Grand Council, in front of which was the large Arsenal, was the building of the Main Guard, built in 1490 for the admiral. There are finely shaped Gothic two-light windows on the first floor. In the 18th century Mario Gropelli changed the entrance portal and mezzanine, giving them baroque characteristics. Beside this building a city belltower with a clock started being built in 1444. In the same year a metal plate for the clock was ordered, and two wooden human figures to strike the hours. Those figure were cast in bronze by an unknown master in 1478, when the clock was renewed and a new bell cast. Today's bell is the work of Ivan of Rab from 1506. The bell-tower leaned sideways badly after the earthquake, and today's was restored after the original in 1929. Simply concieved, it gives a fine accent to the grid-like town plan.

By the bell-tower, between it and Sponza Mansion, is squeezed the Loggia of the bell-ringer. It was built in 1463 to sound the alarm, call the townsmen to hear various proclamations, and it also rang when the councils assembled.

In the 19th century it was destroyed when the headquarters for the Austrian general were built, and was rebuilt in 1952.

The northern side of the square with public and state-administration buildings is closed by Sponza Mansion. Its name comes from the word *spongia* - meaning marsh, which had been here earlier. It was built between 1516 and 1522, after the Senate had accepted the project of the best and most fruitfull Dubrovnik architect Pasko Miličević. The carving was done by the Andrijić brothers.

On the main facade is an arcaded porch holding a terrace. Through it a Gothic portal leads to the inner courtyard. The main facade is richly decorated. The openings on the ground floor, except for the portal, are Renaissance. The first floor is in rich flamboyant Gothic, and the second floor again has simple, but finely profiled Renaissance windows. Between them, in a niche, is a statute of St. Blasius. Above the final cornice is an acroterion. The other facades of this mansion are very simple. The courtyard is a rectuangular atrium with arcades. At the sides were warehouses. Above the groundfloor arcades is a loggia running all the way around, with double pairs of arcades with lancet arches. Above them are the smaller windows of the two next floors.

Between this mansion and the church of St. Blasius, the town patron, stands Orlando's Pillar - the symbol of liberty and independence of medieval mercantile towns. It has a square base, and on it is carved a warrior with a shield and sword. This symbolic pillar was made in 1418 by Antun of Dubrovnik. From it government decisions were proclaimed and celebrations opened. The warrior's right arm, up to his elbow, was Dubrovnik's official measure of length: »one Dubrovnik elbow«.

Between the former buildings of the Arsenal and admiralty, i.e. the Main Guard, is Onforio's Small Fountain. The Napolitan architect Onofrio de la Cava, already mentioned, who was summoned to bring running water into the town, built two especially well-located fountains, Onofrio's Large Fountain on the western beginning of the town and this smaller one, which is a little master-piece of carving skill and gives the most beautiful accent to this square.

In the oldest part of the town, granaries in the form of dry wells are already mentioned quite early.

Today's Rupe Building - Dubrovnik's largest granary - could store large amounts of grain. It was built in the second half of the 16th century. The total capacity of this simple but impossing twostorey building, under which are 15 large dry wells - holes *(Rupa = hole)* is 150 wagons. In the 19th century is lost a floor.

Dubrovnik managed to elevate its ecclesiatical power to the degree of archbishop very early, so as to be less vulnerable from that side also. The first Dubrovnik Cathedral of St. Peter the Great was in the oldest part of the town. Spreading, the town felt the need for a new and larger cathedral and built it close to the state buildings of political power. Thus in 1198, the building of the new Romanesque Cathedral started to the south-west of the Rector's residence - the *kaštel.*

Unfortunately, that magnificent Romanesque building was completely destroyed in the great earthquake. From descriptions of those who had seen it we know that it was really luxuriously decorated with stone lace-like carving. It had five western portals and a large dome. It was correctly sited, and in front of its western facade was an octagonal baptistry built in 1326 of white and red stone. At the beginning it was planned to make it the height of a bell-tower, and for the baptistry to be the ground floor. This monument was also destroyed, not by the earthquake, but thanks to the whim of the Austrian general, who had it knocked down in the 60-ties of the last century to get a better view from his headquarters. Today's Cathedral was built after the earthquake on the site of the Romanesque one, according to plans of the mediocre Roman architect Andrea Bufalini from Urbino. It was built between 1672 and 1713. Its foundation is cruciform, and above the transept is a dome. It is not correctly sited. The portal faces east and the altar west. The decorations of the main facade are somewhat better than those of the other facades, which seem cold and with no inventivity. It is an example of very unsuccessful Roman baroque, and very far from the magnificent old Cathedral. By the Cathedral is the Tresury *(Moćnik).* This is a simple square room with built-in cupboards for the treasures. In it are relics of saints and other objects of great artistic value.

Facing the former Palace of the Grand Council is the church of the town patron St. Blasius, on the site of an older one from 1348, which survived the earthquake. When it burnt down in 1706, today's church of St. Blasius started being built by the Venetian architect Marino Gropelli (built from 1706 to 1714). The church has a square base, and above it rises a central dome. In front of the main facade is an elevated space, from which a wide staircase leads to the square.

The main facade is richly, but rather obtrusively decorated. The side facades are much calmer and simpler. Like the Cathedral, this building too is unsuccessful baroque, and it too is incorrectly sited.

The Jesuit church of St. Ignatius, the most beautiful baroque building in Dubrovnik, is certainly a successful baroque building. It was built at the end of the 17th and the beginning of the 18th century, according to plans of the famous Roman baroque architect and painter Andrea Pozzo. Its main facade faces east and looks onto a large square, which is reached from the lower part of the town by a very lovely baroque stairway, projected in 1738 by the Roman architect Padalaqua. The main facade of the Jesuit church is imposing and skilfully conceived, while the others were neglected. On the north counterforts break up the monotony. It has a square base, a nave and side chapels, is vaulted, and has a semicircular apse. Beside this large church is the baroque building of the former Collegium Ragusinum. The plans were drawn up by Ranjina and Canalia, and it is a large building with an inner courtyard. During the 19th and 20th centuries it was much partitioned.

The most beautiful accent to the entire appearance of the town is given by the two large monasteries with their churches and bell-towers, in the east and west of the town.

In about 1310 the newly-built Dominican Monastery was surrounded by the town walls. Today's monastery church was rebuilt many times. Its quinta-gonal Gothic apse is the oldest part. The church has a nave, and on its southern wall is a rich portal, the work of Bonino of Milan.

The monastery complex has four wings. One of them is the church and the other three are monastery buildings. In the centre these wings form a rectangular cloister, the most valuable and most beautiful part of the monastery.

The Gothic-Renaissance cloister has a rectangular base, and an arcade of triforia. Regardless of Gothic elements and details, the lightness of its arcades gives the cloister a Renaissance atmosphere. It was built in several phases from 1456 to 1469 by local masters, according to the plans of the Florentine Massa.

The bell-tower, basically Romanesque with Gothic elements, was built by local masters between 1404 and 1531. The ground and first floors are part of the monastery, and after the first floor the bell-tower starts to rise independently.

As the Dominican Monastery was built in the eastern part of the town close to the town gates, as if to defend them, so the Franciscan Monastery was built in the west. This monastery complex, whose church burnt down completely in the Great Earthquake, was situated here when the northern part of the town was planned in 1315.

There are two square cloisters, the upper and lower, in the large complex. They also are surrounded by wings of the monastery buildings. The lower cloister, whose southern side leaned on the northern wall of the rebuilt church, is one of the most beautiful works of local architects in the whole of Dubrovnik. It was built by the local master Mihoje Brajkov from Bar, who in 1360 inventively linked late-Romanesque architecture with a Gothic feeling for space.

Double rows of hexaforia separate the covered from the open spaces, enabling sunlight to play freely. To the east of the cloister is the chapter-house, the most beautiful and stylistically purest Renaissance hall in Dubrovnik.

The new church is baroque with no special quality of style and dates from the beginning of the

18th century. On its southern wall is the large Gothic portal, which the earlier church, before the earthquake, had on its western facade. It was made by local masters, the Petrović brothers, in 1498. By Dubrovnik standards it was really luxurious, and shows that the earlier church was much better built than today's.

In 1520 the inhabitants of Dubrovnik built the votive church of the Holy Saviour beside the Franciscan Monastery, after an earthquake which shook the town in that year. It was the work of Korčula masters, the Andrijić brothers. A rare completely preserved work of the Dubrovnik Renaissance, it introduced a new approach and new stylistic elements as yet unused on this soil. The rich but unobtrusive architecture fitted into the space alloted.

Facing the Franciscan Monastery was the large Convent of St. Claire from the 16th century. It had four wings which enclosed a rectangular cloister, and one of which was a church. It lost its original appearance after much Austrian partitioning.

Between those buildings is a small square in whose centre is Onofrio's Large Fountain, erected in 1440, like the other fountains in the town. Apart from its original functionality, the architect of the waterworks made this structure very luxurious and rich. Unfortunately, the Great Earthquake destroyed it, and only its remains show its former functionality and dimensions.

There are many smaller churches and chapels in the town. There are also still-buried ruins of male and female monasteries. They all bore the martk of the time in which they were built.

Apart from mansions, churches and monasteries, there are some other buildings in Dubrovnik which bear special features not only in architecture, but also in the prevailing humane relations towards man. These are in the first place the lazarets. The inhabitants of Dubrovnik very early realized how important quarantine and isolation of people coming from diseased regions was. Earlier than many greater nations they understood the importance of building such buildings. Very little has been preserved of the many smaller lazarets built in the whole Dubrovnik region, only some ruins here and there. Thus there are remains of lazarets on the islet of Bobara, in Danče, Mlini, in Župa etc.

As trade with the east developed, in 1534 the lazaret on Lokrum started being built. It was never finished because the site was too exposed, and there was danger of enemies taking it and attacking the town from a most dangerous point. Later a large building for the quarantine of people and goods was built in the suburb of Ploče. It is a rectangular building divided into five storehouses, with three rooms in each. At the end of each storehouse was a house for the people whose goods were being decontaminated in the storehouse.

This recently restored monument is the best proof of the high consciousness of the Dubrovnik spirit.

The second town of the Republic in strategic and urbanistic value was Ston, both Mali (Small) and Veliki (Large) Ston.

Directly after the purchase of the Pelješac peninsula in 1333, the inhabitants of Dubrovnik decided to fortify the stretch of land dividing the peninsula from the mainland. First they started to build the town of Mali Ston on the small sea (the Neretva canal), and then Veliki Ston. The towns were connected by great defence walls running not only across the stretch of land, but lengthening into two forks towards the top of the mountain and joining at the large fort of Pozvizd, thus forming a single fortification. In the first regulations (1335) concerning the building of both towns a plan was made giving the exact width of streets, sizes of blocks of houses, the placing of public buildings and sewage. Some time later water was brought to the town.

Both small towns were built on sites where there had been nothing before. Furthermore, the earlier classical and early-medieval Ston was in Stonsko polje (the Field of Ston), as can be seen from remains of Roman limitations on the field, and a large number of early-medieval small churches. It was very difficult for the inhabitants of Dubrovnik, almost a whole century after the building of the new towns, to persuade the inhabitants to leave their houses in the field and move into the new settlements.

Dubrovnik's prestige and power among those who had come under them demanded the building of very luxurious public buildings, giving the settlement the mark of a town. The nobles were demanded to build their houses here, which increased the incidence of rich buildings. They built the large Franciscan Monastery, the Bishop's Palace, the Office of the Republic, the Rector's Palace, Cathedral, hospital, public fountain and other public and state buildings.

In Mali Ston are the summer residences of Ston's Vice-Rector, the Bishop and civil servants from Ston.

The independent Ston fortification of Veliki Kaštio was also part of the large fortificational system. It defended Veliki Ston from the sea side, and also the large salt flats, an important factor in the budget of the Republic.

When Dubrovnik became master of Konavli between 1419 and 1427, on the site of destroyed Epidaurum was built the town of Cavtat. This small town on a small peninsula is partly, from the land, surrounded by fortified walls. It was not strictly planned. It was a town of summer houses. Almost every house, poor or rich, has its garden and merges with greenery and flowering trees.

This was also one of the seats of the Vice-Rectorship. The Renaissance palace of the Cavtat Vice-Rectors, in propotion and size, deservs special attention.

The Franciscan Monastery and church were squeezed on the other side of the bay.

At the top of the small hill that dominates the settlement the Mausoleum of the Račić Family was built in the twenties of this century by the outstanding Yugoslav sculptor Ivan Meštrović.

From the end of the 15th century, since many dangers had receded, especially danger of the Turks, the town and state experienced more peaceful times. Townsmen and nobles alike, thirsty for the sun, nature and open spaces, broke out from their protective town to build their homes and mansions, their summer residences, on sites favourable for living.

There are few towns in Dalmatia that had as many summer houses as Dubrovnik. Some were luxurious in architecture, some more modest, but their gardens were always rich, so that often small master-pieces of country architecture were created.

Rijeka Dubrovačka, the Elaphite islands, Pelješac, Orašac, Zaton and other regions of Dubrovnik territory have many summer villas and houses, almost always typical. They are usually a one-storey rectangle with a classical interior distribution: a central hall from which the upper floor is reached, with two rooms on either side. The same distribution is repeated on the first floor. One upper room leads to the terrace or terrace boathouse, which was always part of the living-quarters if the house was close to the sea, thus forming the letter L.

The central hall of the upper storey was for everyday living, for receiving guests and for other more ceremonial occasions. The side rooms were usually bedrooms, and as a fire precaution the kitchen was very often in the loft. Some of the ground-floor rooms served for the storage of agricultural goods, because it must not be forgotten that apart for their love of nature, and the silence and the tranquility of their summer houses, the Dubrovchani here too kept a practical eye on business, being present and overseeing work on the fields, the picking and storage of fruit for their needs and for taxes.

Much would have to be written to present all the more outstanding monuments of Dubrovnik's architectural heritage, like for instance: the fortress-church of the Holy Spirit on Šipan, a fine and specific 16th century building; the lovely monastery, church and fortification complex in Pakljena on Šipan (11th - 16th century); the Benedictine Monastery with a 12th century Romanesque church on Mljet; the settlement of Lopud with highly-decorated houses and mansion, large monasteries and fortifications;

villages and settlements, all of which bear the mark of a special type of Mediterranean architecture.

Dubrovnik emerged from its surrounding soil and spread beyond its fortifications. Architects knew well how to make use of the shape of rocks and the hard land, bearing in mind in the first place the possibility of defense. But at the same time a good relationship with the sea remained, connecting the secure and the beautiful. Bays were inserted into the body of the town, and rocks are the foundations of their building. Building was adapted to nature, technical knowledge was used, but in everything the measure of man was preserved.

A feeling for proportion can be seen in the general, very pure, almost geometrically regular town plan. More outstanding and more ordinary parts of the town succeed each other, and in them the measure of man is always present. This is not by chance.

Dubrovnik is a democratic town, which centred around many and the town community, not some holy ruler or tyrant, who would fashion the town according to his whims. Thus there are no frightening overdimensioned expressions of power, no overcrowding nor exaggerated decoration. There are no devastating differences between the quarters of the rich and the poor, as can often be found in great royal capitals. There is none of that competition often seen in towns, even Mediterranean ones of great esteem, where the whims of the nobles are manifested by clumsy great palaces and towers, which make the rest of the town appear second-rate. In Dubrovnik the Grand Council kept the nobles strictly under the eye and control over their building seems almost like discrimination.

Thus it happened that expression in Dubrovnik was simple, almost the same for all. Roofs with the same cover, slant and cornice; doors and windows almost typical; floors of more or less the same height; material similarily dressed. One man built according to another, and everyone according to all.

Similar needs, opinions, experiences and a feeling for the community linked them, and where that was not so, the ever wakeful government, strict, conscious of its responsibility and size of its task, filled with love for the town, stepped in.

Dubravka Beritić

Painting

Dubrovnik painting is an exceptional chapter in the history of Yugoslav art, and especially in the artistic development of this unique town. Its continuity can be followed from the early Middle Ages until today, and it culminated in the 15th and first decades of the 16th century. It was then that it reached its greatest heights in the works of Lovro Dobričević, Nikola Božidarević and Mihajlo Hamzić.

Only a few remnants of frescoes in pre-Romanesque churches still exist in Dubrovnik and its surroundings. Those that do, in the church of St. Elijah on the island of Lopud, for example, where there is the faded head of a bearded saint with a pall, and yet another saint in the apse, and the remains of recently discovered frescoes in St. Peter and St. Nicholas in Prijeko in Dubrovnik itself, show that even in those days painters decorated the interiors of ecclesiastical buildings.

Two painting on wood have also come down to us from those early centuries. The first is the *Hodigitria Virgin* in the church of St. Andrew in Pile, on which only the heads of the Virgin and Child have been preserved. It shows the fusion of Byzantine and western characteristics, and is rightly dated to the 13th century. The second is the early 14th century *Virgin and Child* in the church of St. Nicholas in Prijeko, which is connected with the famous Zadar painting the *Virgin of the Benedictine Nuns,* and which was added to by a local painter in the 16th century.

The Cathedral frescoes, begun in 1313 by Michele of Bologna, who had moved to Dubrovnik, were destroyed in the 1667 earthquake and disappeared without trace, together with the old Romanesque Cathedral. In 1318 Michele was commissioned for further work in the Cathedral, and to paint the miniatures in an antiphonal. In 1324 he decorated the apse of the church of St. Stephen, and in 1344 painted the decorations in the hall of the Grand Council. We can suppose that this artist, who came from the then exceptionally flourishing Emilian centre of painting, played an important role in Dubrovnik painting in the first half of the 14th century. The painters Bernardo (1345), Misole of Zadar (1348) and Marko of Apulia (1351) were also in Dubrovnik at that time, but we know nothing more about them.

Some time later Dubrovnik documents mention three painters who were obviously Byzantine Emanual the Greek (1367), George the Greek (1377-1386) and Joan from Dürres (1388-1389). They belonged to the group of so-called *pictores graeci,* and played a certain role in events that took place at the end of the 14th century in Adriatic towns from Zadar to Kotor.

Pre-Romanesque painters in Dubrovnik are largely unknown, but documents show clearly that in the 14th century foreign artists were predominant. The first documented generation of local Dubrovnik painters appeared at the end of that century in connection with the workshop of another artist from Bologna, Francesco di Nani, who made and decorated in painting luxurious shields. Painters from the Frušković and Ivanović families were especially outstanding in Nani's *bottega,* and they later opened their own workshops in which the craft was carried for several generations. Their works seem not to have gone beyond the restrictions of artistic craftsmanship.

They painted decorations on shields, decorated carved chests and materials for curtains, and even walls in homes.

The first important Dubrovnik painter was Blaž Jurjev. He came to Dubrovnik from his hometown Trogir, which shows the artistic links that existed between Dalmatian towns.

This painter of gentle Virgins with unusual and seemingly sickly eyes, young saints depicted as elegant knights and dark-skinned old saints, frowning and stern, was one of the greatest figures of the »Dalmatian school of painting«. He worked in Dubrovnik from 1421 to 1427. Witness of his stay in the town of St. Blasius, where he even became the official painter of the Republic, are the damaged Madonna in the church of St. George in Boninovo and the exceptional crucifixion in the Ston Monastery of St. Nicholas.

These works, and also his later paintings throughout Dalmatia, evince a subtle late-Gothic expression with a very personal style and use of colour, and a use of line that can only be called witty. A distinctive feature of this artist can be seen in the musical cadences of the folds of gowns and cloaks.

For some time longer the inhabitants of Dubrovnik entrusted all really important commissions to foreigners (Antonio di Jacopo of Lucca painted new frescoes in the Cathedral, and Lorenzo di Michele of Florence the interior of the hall of the Small Council). After that local artists took all the main positions in painting. The period from the end of the 14th century may be considered a specific Dubrovnik variant of the »Dalmatian school of painting«. That rich period in the painting of the Adriatic coast has all the essential characteristics that modern history of art demands in order to recognize a »school«: a large number of local artists; mutual interconnections; a craft carried down from generation to generation; scope and quality of painting; local characteristics and common factors of influence. Dubrovnik in its special context is an exceptional and special chapter because of many special characteristics, of the unique heights it achived during the Renaissance, and because of the length of time that the local school lasted. It continued for over half a century longer than in the other towns from Zadar to Kotor, which were under Venetian rule.

The first outstanding artist, who can be considered to have originated from Dubrovnik itself, was Ivan Ugrinović at the beginning of the third decade of the 15th century. Numerous documents record his many commissions and great number of associates, but all that remains of his fruitful activity are the signed miniature with the figure of St. Blasius in the manuscript of the Dubrovnik Statues, and the polyptych in the church of St. Anthony in Koločep, connected with him on the basis of a 1434 document which asys that he was to paint a polyptych for that forested islet of the Elaphite archipelago. On the basis of those works Ugrinović seems to have been a step backwards with regard to Blaž Jurjev, because his works were still greatly under the influence of Venetian painting of the second half of the 14th century, especially that of Paolo and Lorenzo Veneziano,

their followers Caterino and Donato, and other masters of that circle. The Institute for the Preservation of Cultural Monuments in Dubrovnik has recently discovered fragments of frescoes in the church of St. Nicholas in Prijeko, which could be by Ugrinović. But they are unfortunately insufficient to illustrate with any clarity his physiognomy as a painter of large wall compositions, or to give us any definite confirmation of his painting personality.

Matko Jurković, who came to Dubrovnik from Kotor in 1448, also shows conservative and back-looking characteristics, not only in regard to contemporary Venetian and Italian painting in general, but also in regard to painting in the other coastal towns of the eastern Adriatic coast. Death inturrupted his work early, in 1454. His only preserved work is the dissembled polyptych in the church of Our Lady of Šunj on Lopud, attributed on the basis of a 1452 document. This work still shows the influence of late 14th century Venetian ideals, although some details have the breath of the Gothic style.

Several more paintings by as yet unidentified painters, and remains of rare faded frescoes, show the gradual adoption of the Gothic style in Dubrovnik painting. This would surely be clearer today if most of the works had not been destroyed for ever in fires and earthquakes and because their importance was not realized in earlier centuries.

Those losses are to be compensated for by the preserved works of the most important painter in quality, up-to-dateness and importance who worked in Dubrovnik in the middle and the third quarter of the 15th century: Lovro Dobričević Marinov.

This artist was first mentioned in a 1444 Venetian document together with the outstanding Venetian painter Michele Giambono, who was probably his teacher. He returned first to his birthplace Kotor, and then came to Dubrovnik, where he worked from 1459 to 1478.

We shall limit ourselves here only to three of his works in Dubrovnik: the 1448 polyptych in the Dominican Monastery, on which he collaborated with Matko Junčić, who probably carved the intricate frame; the 1455-58 panel with the figure of St. Blasius in the polyptych for the church of the Little Brothers; and the 1465-66 polyptych from the church of Our Lady in Dančе. They show clearly the importance of his personality and the characteristics of his style.

The Baptism is central to the composition in the Dominican church. The Madonna with a mandorla of cobalt-blue angels is painted lyrically, and beside her the elegant figures of St. Michael and St. Lawrence. It is still close to the spirit of late Gothic vision, discreetly interwoven with echoes of a familiarity with early works by Antonio Vivarini.

The panel with St. Blasius reveals a step forward towards new aspirations in a much more plastic conception, softer modellation and a fresher treatment of colour. It leads logically to the polyptych in Dančе, showing a Virgin with a melancholy face and blue cloak, beneath which two angels play their instruments, while the Holy Father is surrounded by angels painted in an intense scale of red and orange shades. The figure of the gentle and spiritual St. Julian, although predominantly in refined late-Gothic expression, reveals the presence of as yet subdued, but already felt Renaissance characteristics, in a still more expressive treatment of volume, soft modulation, stressed individuality, a more sparing use of gold, and treatment of colour.

In the second half of the 15th century many other painters, whose works have not been preserved or are as yet unidentified, worked in Dubrovnik. A special place among them is held by Ugrinović's heirs, outstanding among whom is Stjepan. To him are hypothetically attributed the paintings of the Virgin from the church of St. Jacob on Peline; and the Ognjanović family, whose members were artists for several generations.

The last decade of the 15th and the beginning of the 16th century were a turning-point, and very important for the history of old Dubrovnik painting. Most important were three artists: Vicko, son of Lovro Dobričević, and to a much greater degree, Nikola Božidarević and Mihajlo Hamzić.

Of that trio Vicko Lovrin was most tied by tradition. His 1509-1510 polyptych in the Franciscan church in Cavtat, with the large figure of St. Michael in gold armour, is still painted in conservative schemes and framework, although some of its details, especially the Virgin and saints on the gable, show that he obviously knew Venetian painting of the late 15th century, and especially that of Bartolomeo Vivarini, with whose painting undoubtable analogies can be seen.

Nikola Božidarević is the most important painter in all of old Dubrovnik painting. His father was the painter Božidar Vlatković, considered to be the author of the damaged Virgin in the ruined polyptych on the main altar of Cavtat's Franciscan church. Nikola Božidarević was first mentioned in 1476 in the workshop of Petar Ognjanović. The following year he went to study in Venice. After a long period spent in Italy, during which, as we can conclude from preserved works, he obviously travelled the Marches after studying among the lagoons, and perhaps went to Umbria and Rome, he again came to Dubrovnik in 1494. At first he collaborated with his father, and after 1497 worked independently. Of a large number of works mentioned in documents, four that are in a sufficient state of preservation illustrate the profile of his artistic personality.

Božidarević's oldest extant work is the triptych in Bundić's chapel in the Dominican church. Stylistic analysis and the faithful model of the town held by St. Blasius, allow us to date this painting to the beginning of the 16th century. The artist still followed the traditional form of the triptych and used a gold background, but the plasticity and vitality of the figures, the classical symmetry of the composition and the floor, painted in perspective, already show Renaissance characteristics.

On *The Annunciation,* painted in 1513 by order of the seaman Marko Kolendić for the Lopud Dominicans, we have in fact the oldest preserved large scene painted for a church in Dubrovnik painting. The feeling for space was achieved by the plastic figures of the protagonists and the manycoloured horizontal planes which stress the depth of the landscape, with picturesque wooded islands and blueish mountains. A new spirit seems to spring from the reddish porch and circular building, woven into the landscape of that painting, under which is a predella with livelly scenes which intertwine Biblical themes and scenes from everyday life. In the same year, 1513, Božidarević was commissioned by the Đorđić family to execute a painting for the chapter-house in the Dominican Monastery, on which he accepted completely the *Sacra conversazione* motif. Especially outstanding in this work, on whose gable is an inspired scene of the Deposition, is the lyrical figure of the Virgin. Here he gave an exceptional realization of this ideal of womanhood, the dreamy figure of St. Julian and the spiritual St. Jacob. The kneeling donor, discovered during recent restoration, must also be mentioned.

On the 1517 polyptych in the church of Our Lady at Dance Božidarević, bowing to the desire of those who commissioned it, returned to the traditional scheme of the polyptych, but he knew how to unite the separate panels into a unity. On this masterpiece, which he painted shortly before his death, must be mentioned the figure of the old St. Gregory and the young, pale St. Martin on horseback, the »surrealiste« scene of St. George slaying the dragon in an illuminated landscape filled with skulls, and the scene of Golgotha on the lunette.

If we look at his work as a whole, Božidarević represents the synthesis and culmination of old Dubrovnik painting. He links traditions of the local school with echoes of the new Renaissance spirit and expresses a personal note in the choice of colour, typology and composition. In his paintings Božidarević realized an expressively personal interpretation of the Renaissance vision of painting, in which can be felt the land and climate from which he stemmed, and the new revolutionary concepts of space and volume which became predominant in the 15th century in west-European art.

Mihajlo Hamzić, the youngest of the trio, is mentioned for the first time in a 1509 document in which the Senate accepts his painting of St. John the Baptist, and from which we can conclude that he studied painting with Andrea Mantegna. To that document is also connected the large painting of *The Baptism* in the Rector's Palace, which is the oldest preserved large composition in free space in old Dubrovnik art. It shows three bony protagonists, Christ, St. John the Baptist and the angel, in a spaceous rocky landscape painted in gradations of brown and green. Here can be seen Hamzić's great knowledge of aerial perspective, enlivened with many picturesque details.

While the expressive key to *The Baptism* is in the use of shading, the second work of this fine Renaissance painter, Lukarević's triptych in the Dominican church (1512), is predominantly colouristic. In external form we can note a similarity with Božidarević. After his spacious composition in the open, this return to a more traditional scheme was obviously at the desire of the local donor.

Here too Hamzić did not hide his stylistic origins stemming from Mantegna, but he also revealed a much greater closeness to Venetian painting. He could have come to know this either through his assistant and co-worker Pier Giovannini from Venice, who came to his workshop in 1512 from Recanati, or from any of his visits to Venice where he went on business, in which he was much more active than in painting.

The deaths of Nikola Božidarević at the end of 1517 (or in early 1518), Vicko Lovrin Dobričević in 1517-1518 and Mihajlo Hamzić in 1518 seem symbolically to mark the end of the culmination of old Dubrovnik painting and the beginning of its decline.

Although we can follow a continuity of art in Dubrovnik for almost half a century, it was not even the shadow of its earlier quality and creativity. Some of the more important reasons for the gradual agony of the school were the increase of direct imports from Italy, and even the Flanders, the demand of educated patrons, who commissioned from artists paintings in the spirit of the new times, or, on the contrary, the conservative tendencies of the few remaining local painters, and the coming of many mediocre painters from Italy to Dubrovnik.

The most important of those comers from Italy was certainly the already mentioned Pier Giovannini from Venice. After Hamzić's death he opened an independent workshop in Dubrovnik and during half a century of activity painted many paintings for the town and surroundings. His preserved paintings, for instance the polyptych in the church of Our Lady of the Cave in Lopud, the triptych in the Lopud Parish Museum or the paintings in the church of St. Andrew in Pile show that he had become completely local, because together with many Venetian influences and components we can also see on them many retarded provincial characteristics. I would also mention the painter Pier Antonio Palmerini from Urbino, who spent several years in Dubrovnik in the second half of the third decade of the 16th century. On his altarpiece *The Ascension* in the church of the Holy Saviour, and on the painted cupboard-retable in the sacristy of the Little Brothers, we sense reflections of the Urbino circle of painting from the end of the 15th century, and paler reminiscences of the painting of his great compatriot Raphael.

In this period local painters can be divided into three groups.

The first, in fact, continued the local tradition, trying to connect an out-lived heritage from the past with modest echoes of new currents. Rare preserved works in Dubrovnik, Šipan and Lastovo cannot with certainty be linked with the many names of local artists named by documents as active in the town and surroundings in the second quarter and in the middle of the 16th century (Petar Bogdanović, Stjepan Radovanović, Petar Radonjić, Marko Radojević etc.).

The second group returned to Bytantium for inspiration, especially to works by Cretan-Venetian masters, some of whom probably worked in Dubrovnik (Angelos and Donato Bizanano). Icons by others came to the town from their workshops on the far away island in the middle of the Mediterranean, from Apulia and from the lagoons. The main artist of this group is considered to be Franjo Matijin, to whom the triptych in the church of St. Stephen in Sustjepan in Rijeka dubrovačka is attributed. Byzantine charac-

teristics can be seen here in the hierarchal and stylized saintly figures, in manner of shading and modelling, in the renewed use of gold backrounds, in the relationship between colours and in Greek inscriptions. Together with those elements the artist also introduced some types used by Catholic iconography, and certain latent stylistic detals show that he was familiar with western painting. Several more paintings are connected with the artist, or to be more precise, with his workshop.

Some icons of the Virgin and Child in Dubrovnik and its surroundings, however, in their connection of Cretan-Venetian schemes and local western elements, reveal that they were painted by local artists of similar tendencies.

The third group, which appeared some time later, is characterized by direct imitation of imported paintings by masters of the Venetian 16th century, but with no understanding of their artistic essence. The most typical representative here was Kristofor Antunović Nikolin, whose 1552 polyptych in the Pakljeni church on Šipan imitates to a high degree the polyptych of Titian and his workshop, today in Dubrovnik Cathedral. But this mediocre local artist could not fathom the core of the artistic message imparted by the great Venetian.

Here we must also mention the painter Vlaho Držić (1503-1570), son of a prominent Dubrovnik family and brother of the great playwright. He was closely connected with outstanding Italian and Dubrovnik writers, but the problem of his artistic work is still an open question in the history of art.

In the seventies of the 16th century the Dubrovnik variant of Dalmatian art completely ceased to exist. During the mannerist, baroque and classicist periods only individual isolated local and foreign painters of little merit worked in the town, and imported paintings only partially substituted for the fruitful activity of local workshops, as the conditions under which they had formerly flourished ended.

Pellegrino Brocardo from Ventimiglia especially represented mannerist currents. He came to Dubrovnik as the personal painter of the Dubrovnik

Archbishop, writer and fried of Titian and Michelangelo, Ludovico Boccadelli (1556-1564).

His altarpiece showing St. Matthew has been preserved in the Dubrovnik Cathedral. He decorated the Archbishop's summer mansion on Šipan with frescoes. They are in part preserved, and show mythological-allegoric scenes and portraits of famous personages, including Michelangelo. In Brocardo's work can be felt the influence of Florentine mannerism. This can also be found on the altarpece of the Dominican church, *The Descent of the Holy Spirit*, by Bronzino's pupil Santi di Tito, which shows a portrait of the donor Vice Stjepović Skočibuha.

Mentioning this art we cannot, at the end of this short survey of painting in Dubrovnik until the end of the 16th century, bypass some of the most important imported works by foreign old masters, which have become part of the Yugoslav artistic inventory, proving the high cultural level of those who ordered them. In the first place must be mentioned the great Crucifixion from the beginning of the second half of the 14th century by Paolo Veneziano in the Dominican church, and also two works by Titian: the polyptych from the beginning of the fifth decade of the 16th century painted by that artist and his assistants for the church of St. Lazarus in Ploče (today behind the main altar in the Cathedral), and the altarpiece *St. Magdalene,* painted for the Dominican church after the middle of the century. According to tradition, it also shows the figure of the donor, the Dubrovnik noble Damjan Pucić. Outstanding among works by Italian masters are also Giambono's *Madonna* in the Historical Institute of the Yugoslav Academy, Christ's figure by a central-Italian master from the second half of the 15th century (attributed to Francesco Francia) with the Little Brothers, the tondo *The Holy Family* by the workshop of Lorenzo di Credi with the Dominicans, *Venus and Adonis* by Paris Bordone in the Rector's Palace, and several paintings in the Cathedral which, true, did not come to Dubrovnik until 1713, after the donation by the canon Bernardo Đorđić from the so-called »heritage of Paspi« (Palma Vecchio, Paris Bordone, Padovanino, Savoldo etc.). A special place among imported works is held by Flemish paintings: the triptych *The* *Adoration of the Magi* in the Cathedral treasury shows the influence of Hans Memling; the diptych showing *Christ and the Virgin* in the Dominican Monastery, several replicas and variants of which exist in European and and American museums, can be ascribed to a Flemish workshop from the second half af the 15th century; the painting in the church in Pakljena near Suđurađ on Šipan, with a lovely landscape in the background, is the work of an Antwerp workshop from the second quarter of the 16th century.

These works by outstanding foreign painters, today in Dubrovnik, are known throughout the world both to experts and the public. Yugoslav and foreign art historians have examined them and written studies about them, and they are important not only in Dubrovnik, but also in the whole of the Yugoslav artistic heritage.

During the baroque period there were several Dubrovnik painters of lesser importance. Nothing has come down to us by Ignac Martellini (1624-1656) or Grgur Ivanelić (1690- ?). The charming alterpiece *The Annunciation* in the Cathedral is with great probability attributed to Benko Stay (1650-1687), to whom Petar Kanavelić dedicated a song urging him to paint the victory of Jan Sobieski under Vienna. The most prolific and most important local painter was Petar Mattei-Matejević (1670-1726), who first studied painting with Stay, and then specialized in Venice and Naples. His Venetian and Napolitan experiences can be felt in his main works: the altarpiece *St Bernardo before the Virgin* in the Cathedral, the large allegoric compositions of the apotheosis of Faith and Martyrdom in the Cathedral treasury, and the cycle of smaller paintings on the balustrade of the organ in the church of St. Blasius *(sv. Vlaho)*.

The greatest cycle of baroque paintings in Dubrovnik was by a painter of Spanish origin Gaetano Garcia, pupil of Solimena in Naples. He came to Dubrovnik from Palermo and in 1737-38 decorated the apse of the Jesuit church with scenes from the life of St. Ignatius Loyola. Those frescoes, whose compositions are in most cases copied from the works of contemporary artists, cannot be denied skilful excution and a feeling for the spirit of baroque decoration of church interiors, full of emphatic pathos, ringing colours and dynamic light effects.

Imported baroque shows a strong connection between Dubrovnik and the painting of central and southern Italy (altarpieces by A. Vaccara, G. Imparata, F. de Maria, G. A. Canini etc. in Dubrovnik, and by G. Lanfranca in Lastovo), although works by Venetian artists can still be found. Outstanding among them is the altarpiece by S. Ricci in the Carmen church and the painting by F. Zugno with the Dominicans.

Connections with Rome can be seen during the short classicist period, which is in fact the only chapter of classicist art in Dalmatia. Dubrovnik had two classicist painters, Petar Katušić (1767-1788) and Rafo Martini (1771-1846), and they both studied at the expense of the Republic with Mengs' pupil Antonio Maroni. Katušić died very young. Martini painted portraits of prominent Dubrovnik citizens (D. Restić, F.M. Appendini) best among which is the water-colour of P.F. Papis in the Dubrovnik Haller Collection. Carmelo Reggio (?-1819) from Palermo, who had also studied in Rome, worked in Dubrovnik during the first two decades of the 19th century. He painted many mediocre paintings of sacral motifs, and many portraits in which he achieved his highest level, leaving in his portraits of members of the Stulli, Andrović and Chersa families a gallery of the most important Dubrovnik personalities at the moment when Napoleon stifled the liberty of the Republic.

After an almost complete end of painting activity lasting for over half a century, in the last quarter of the 19th century Dubrovnik again produced an important painter: Vlaho Bukovac (1855-1922) of Cavtat. At first he painted in the spirit of Parisian academism, but later used lighter colours, went through a short meeting with symbolistic currents, then took over certain *plein-air* characteristics, and finally divisionist tendencies. After a tempestous youth spent as a sailor, he studied and lived first in Paris, often returning to his homeland, and then spent most of his life in Zagreb, Cavtat and Prague. His role as a painter, organizer and teacher had a great influence on the beginnings of more recent Croatian painting.

Between the two wars the greatest Dubrovnik painter was Ignat Job (1895-1936). Through the intense colours of his palette and prism of a frenetic expressionism he realized his vision of the landscape and people of Dalmatia, permeated with sun, light and the joy of life, and rich with an expressive and dynamic personal temperament. At that time Dubrovnik more and more became the inspiration of a whole series of artists from many Yugoslav centres. Outstanding in the town itself as an individual personality was especially Gabro Rajčević (1912-1943), whose canvases were first heavily impasted in light colours, which later became more serene and in a darker gamut. His work, full of promise, was interrupted by his untimely death.

After the liberation Dubrovnik painting again fluorished through the activites of many interesting painters who were, each in his own way, inspired by the specific atmosphere, ambience and colours of this town, in which they were born or worked. Untimely death broke off the lives and artistic work of Antun Masle (1919-1967), a painter of a swinging gamut of colours and a specific poetry with a characteristic vision of the world in which echoes a note of chidlike joy; and Ivo Dulčić (1916-1975), an inspiered and deep colourist of exceptional strength who, in his oils, frescoes and painting on glass (outstanding among those in Dubrovnik are the ones on the windows of the church of St. Blasius), showed himself to be a great figure in modern Croatian painting. The most prominent of the still living and active painters working in Dubrovnik today, since it is impossible to list them all in this short survey, are Branko Kovačević (1911), Đuro Pulitika (1922), Ivo Vojvodić (1923), Mladen Pejaković (1928), Milovan Stanić (1929), Ivo Grbić (1931), Lukša Peko (1941) and Josip Škerlj (1941). Many have a reputation far beyond the boundaries of their town and bear witness to the continuity, vitality and universality of Dubrovnik as an art centre, which continues in present-day language the great and unbroken tradition of centuries gone by, recounted in this short survey.

Kruno Prijatelj

Craftwork in Dubrovnik

The goldsmiths and silversmiths, known as »fine craftsmen«, were organized into socially, politically and economically well-developed societies. Costly materials like gold and silver, from which articles for church or lay use were made, and often also gilded copper, were so expensive that they demanded economically highly organized societies, able to develop a market. This created conditions for the development of local goldsmiths' and silversmiths' crafts. Thus we only find local gold and silverwork in economically, socially and politically advanced regions in Croatia: in Dubrovnik, Zadar, Trogir and Split in Dalmatia, and in the continental part of Croatia in Zagreb, Varaždin and some smaller goldwork centres - Osijek and Slavonska Požega.

The astute leaders of the Dubrovnik Republic valued the goldsmiths highly, accorded them special privileges and aided and protected their local products, paying special attention to competition and imports from abroad. The Republic of St. Blasius exported the works of local goldsmiths, thus strengthening and spreading its trade in gold and silver objects, which played a very important role in its economy. Very early there was strict control over the purity of silver (in 1277) and gold (regulations from 1352, 1666 and 1773).

From the 15th century onwards the hallmark of the Republic, which was the head of St. Blasius in a Bishop's mitre, was obligatory as a guarantee of the high quality of gold and silverwork. The craftsmen's hallmark was also obligatory.

From the 13th century the Republic of St. Blasius also minted its own money in its mint in the Divona or Sponza Mansion. The Dubrovnik mint started in 1294 (copper money, so-called *folari*), and from 1337 to 1803 Dubrovnik's own copper and silver coins were minted without a break.

Local gold and silversmiths cut the dies. Most famous among them was the medallist Pavko Antonijević (Pavao Dubrovčan), assistant of Donatello in Italy, who worked in Dubrovnik from 1461.

Local Dubrovnik gold and silversmiths did not engrave dies for the Dubrovnik Republic only during the most glorious days of its history, i.e. from the 13th to the 16th century, but later also - in the 17th and 18th century, until the fall of the Republic. They also engraved dies for the mints in Kotor and Ulcinj (Kristofor Marinov).

Dubrovnik goldsmiths were united in a special brotherhood by 1306. All the rules regarding the social and economic position, and the rights and duties of its members, were given in great detail. The society also provided a kind of »social insurance« in the event of the illness of a member or of his family. They had their street in Dubrovnik, which is still called Zlatarska (Goldsmiths'), and in which were situated their workshops and houses.

During the most glorious period in the development of goldwork in Dubrovnik (i.e. from the 13th the 16th century) there were many gold and silversmiths in the town, who made church vessels and objects for secular use (tableware, jewelry etc.). For instance, the 13th century goldsmith Pavle made the gilded silver ciborium for the Dubrovnik Cathedral. In the second half of the same century we know of the local masters Prvonja, Vasilij, Maroje, Krasin Dešimirov, Radomir Korljić and others, whose names and surnames prove their Croatian origin.

In the 14th century the master-craftsmen Pasko Radičev, Gjivo Prodanov, Utješen Klapčić and others worked in Dubrovnik. Outstanding among local masters were Ivan Progonović and the medallist Pavao Dubrovčan (Pavko Antonijević), and in the 16th century Jerolim Matov and Marulo Joanneo.

As has already been said, the most important and creative period of Dubrovnik gold and silverwork was from the 13th to the 16th century. However, the archives show that many local masters worked in Dubrovnik in the 17th and 18th centuries too, although after the fall of Bosnia and Serbia under the Turks the influx of siver from Bosnian and Serbian silvermines into Dubrovnik decreased. Those masters mostly made jewelry, but they also made church vessels for the use of the Republic's churches and monasteries, a small number of which are still kept in ecclesiastical treasuries on the territory of the former Republic of St. Blasius. We shall mention only some names from that period, for instance: in the 17th century Kristofor Marinov, Andree di Giugliano, Sebastiano Gentili, Dimitar Petrović, Ivan Kimak, Francesco Ferro, and in the 18th century Ivan Luić, Florio Martinović, Nikola Čingris, Kristo Jerinić, Matteo Fišić

Unfortunately, most of both older and more recent Dubrovnik secular gold and silverwork has disappeared during the centuries, since it was much in use, and often changed owners. What can still be found in Dubrovnik can only fragmetarily show all the diversity and skill of local masters, whose activities, as we can see, can be followed until the 19th century.

A far greater number of gold and silver objects from the same period, 13th to 19th century, made for use in churches have been preserved. They can be found in church and monastery treasuries in Dubrovnik and the whole territoty of the Republic. Those objects, made by local and localized Dubrovnik masters, and kept in treasuries for centuries, did not change owners so often. Thus it is only through them, and also on the basis of objects imported into the town, that we can today get at least an approximate picture of the richness, value and scope not only of local gold craftwork from the 13th to the 19th century, but also of the degree of culture and economic development of Dubrovnik society.

The treasury of the Dubrovnik Cathedral has the oldest and most valuable examples not only of Dubrovnik, but also of foreign silver and goldwork from the 13th to the 18th century.There is the reliquary Hand of St. Blasius (gilded silver decorated with cloisonne enamel, 11th-12th century); the reliquary Head of St. Blasius (also decorated with cloisonne enamel, 11th-12th century); the silver reliquary of St. Lawrence from 1348, by the master Guglielmo; the late-Gothic reliquary Hand of St. Petar from the 15th century; the late-Renaissance silver ewer and tray decorated with plants and animals, from the Nurenberg Jamnitzer workshop (16th century); the gilded silver cross with a wooden relic from the Holy Cross, by the Dubrovnik master Jerolim Matov, about 1536; and the gilded silver

reliquary Foot of St. Blasius, 1684. Some ecclesiastical works from Venetian and Roman silversmiths' workshops from the 17th and 18th centuries have also been preserved.

The treasury of the Dubrovnik church of St. Blasius has the old silver and gilt statue of the town patron, St. Blasius, with a model of the town in his hand (mid-15th century).

There are also 17th and 18th century Italian church vesels. In the treasury of the Franciscan Monastery is the silver and gilt reliquary of the figures of SS. Sergius and Vladislav from the second half of the 15th century, and a silver cross by the master-craftsman Hans of Basel (from 1440). Of more recent works there are some church vessels by local Dubrovnik masters, church vessels by foreign masters, predominantly Venetian, and some works by Viennese silversmiths from the end of the 18th century.

The most important examples of Dubrovnik and foreign 13th to 18th century silverwork are exibited in the treasury of the Dominican Monastery. Outstanding among them is an ostensory with a Gothic stand and a more recent upper part. A censor in the form of a Dubrovnik *karaka* (type of ship), identical in shape with that shown on *The Annunciation* by the Dubrovnik painter Nikola Božidarević, is probably the work of a Dubrovnik master, like the ostensory.

Among older objects in the treasury of that monastery is a simply made silver cross, commissioned by the Serbian King Uroš Milutin for the church of SS. Peter and Paul, which was probably brought to Dubrovnik after the fall of Serbia under the Turks. Outstanding among 17th and 18th century gold and silverwork is that by local Dubrovnik masters (church vessels), and some Venetian and Viennese church vessels. An important collection of church vessels, representing Roman and Venetian masters from the end of the 17th and the 18th century, is kept in the sacristy of the Dubrovnik Jesuit church.

In the small church in Dance there are small 15th to 19th century silver votive plaques.

Outside the town itself we find many important works by Dubrovnik and foreign masters from the 13th to the 18th century. In the parish church and museum in Lopud are a chalice with angels, a *patena* and ostensory of gilded silver from the 15th century, many 16th to 19th century votive plaques, and works by Italian masters from the 17th and 18th centuries.

Many other ecclesiastical buildings on the territory of the former Dubrovnik Republic also have individual objects by Dubrovnik and Venetian silversmiths. Important, for instance, is the collection in the Franciscan Monastery in Kuna and Orebić on the Pelješac peninsula, and that in the Cavtat parish church.

The many masters of artistic gold and silverwork, who made their objects for the needs of the Dubrovnik Republic, its nobles, citizens, churches and monasteries between the 13th and the 19th century, that is until the fall of the Republic of St. Blasius (1808), and even later, during Austrian rule, brought the craft to a high artistic level and beauty. Their great skill and the fineness and harmony of their works were the reason that most them disappeared during the 19th, and especially in the 20th century.

This treasure was dispersed, mostly unrecognized, among museums and collections throughout Europe and the world.

Ivo Lentić

On the Literary Paths of Dubrovnik

»...New spring for me
is crowned with varied flowers;
frutiful summer
fills fields with golden ears;
ripe autumn
is decorate with fruit.

Winter for me means fire struck from flint,
wood from the mountain;
for me old mother fills her skirt
with fruitful gift of seeds;
for me fish glide
from the sea and from water;

For me the bird nests,
the bee gathers honey,
the sheep outspreads her fleece,
the ox labours at the yoke for me,
black horses ride,
the sun, the moon and the stars shine.«

(Ivan F. Gundulić)

Thousands of pages of affection and enthusiasm could be written about Dubrovnik's old literature, about its first poets Džore Držić and Šiško Menčetić, about Dinko Ranjina, Dominik Zlatarić, Sabo Bobaljević, Mavro Vetranić, Antun Sasina, Nikola Dimitrović, Nikola Nalješković, Andrija Čubranović Zlatar, Cvijeta Zuzorić and many others of the 15th and 16th centuries, about the Renaissance of Marin Držić, his comedies which lit the immortal torch of laughter, about the genius of Dživo Fran Gundulić, the peerless writer of *Osman*, an epic poem whose poetic image of the 17th century has remained untouched until today, and whose creator became one of the greatest men of world literature, about the tragedy of more recent writers, who lived after the fall of the Dubrovnik Republic: Vojnović, Vodopić, Kosor.

All of these, and many other artists, are the immortal glory of Dubrovnik, its most illustrous pages. They are the links which connect present and future in a living and unbroken chain. They were the first in Europe to celebrate a literary republic, they left a permanent record of invaluable works. They were the first in Croatian history to write, in great numbers, in the spirit of the people, and to write creative work for the people and the ordinary man, work that grew out of the native soil. They formed the strong basis of Croatian literature and have their place in South Slav, Slav, and even world literature.

In Široka ulica no. 19 stands a small, unassuming house, an ordinary two-storey town house. It has no south wall, but adjoins the church of Domina. In it lived the poet Džore Držić and his nephew the playwright Marin Držić, literary masters of 16th century Dubrovnik.

From this small home took flight the magnificent Dubrovnik eagle, Marin Držić, an ordinary man and citizen, yet a giant of the pen, the glory and pride of Dubrovnik, the crown of Renaissance Dubrovnik and with a well-marked place among world comedy writers. The memorial plaque above the two small windows shows the year of his birth (1507) and his death (1567). Hardship, suffering, injustice, a visionary eye, an artistic and tortured spirit. He presented comic portraits of his contemporaries and co-citizens, and ended with works of biting and yet victorious laughter, alternately scourge and balm. He cut his life by half. In the dark grey house, half swallowed by the Domina church, it seems that the window frame moves, that a bending figure watches from behind the church corner. The figure is very grave and does not laugh, but moves with dignity. Across the streets from Puč and Gundulićeva Poljana it comes in front of the Rector's Palace. In its hands is no paper nor ink:

»Noble and gracious gathering, folk ancient and wise, I see how with ears intent and eyes filled with curiosity you stand in expectation of hearing and seeing this evening some fair thing; and I believe, if I do not deceive myself, that you think and hope some truly excellent thing to behold, but truly excellent things have not in these parts until now been performed!«

The »Pomet Group« is giving a carnival performance of *Uncle Maroje (Dundo Maroje).* We listen to the ringing and triuphant voice of Pomet: »... And more I will not say, but will beg you with kindness in your hearts to listen and see, for if you grow to liking us then we and our things will be dear to you, but if otherwise even a fair comedy will seem to you ugly which will be not the play's fault but your own ... But here is Uncle Maroje, put all your wits now into this our play. And Good-bye.«

Immortal figures pass before the stage setting known as »Before the Rector's Palace«. Laughter is caught between tragedy and humour, comic portraits reach the culmination of realization, true life starts roaring out again in front of locked doors, the demons of injustice leave the stage to the goddess of justice, Marin Držić is triumphant. Life can flow every way, Držić's genius only clothes it, comedy accompanies him on the eternal battlefield. Dubrovnik stages encompass the seas, the world, widespread towns, sometimes even Rome.

The playwright Držić, humanist and Latinist, expert in the Dubrovnik variant of Croatian, which was his mother tongue, one of the typically versatile personalities of the European Renaissance, predecessor of Molière and Cervantes, contemporary of Rebelais, student and vice-rector of the university of Siena, brought Dubrovnik Renaissance comedy to its apex. His Bokčilo, enriched by the sap of hunger like Gargantua, is immortal.

Pomet is the greatest figure of this work, and Pomet was also the name of the acting company, he is Marin Držić himself, master of all situations on the stage and in life. In him lives the omnipotent genius of Marin Držić, and he is invincible.

Through the character of Pomet this great Dubrovnik writer put everyone in his place, from prince to servant. His humour is a needle piercing vice and evil to the very heart.

Those he studies and places under the magnifying glass of his comedies feel uneasy. »Someone has done something original, and who but Pomet.« Popiva, Tudeško, Skup, Maroje, Maro and many others from Dubrovnik, and outside it, called him a »traitor«, to which he serenely answered, with the sting of truth: »the more right you are, the more wrong.«

Držić's comedy raised the dust widely, it was like a revolution in literature and the comic portrayal of persons.

And here is the »Njarnjas Company«. The spectators sit where today is Placa, Stradun. Around them the Sponza, the Rector's Palace, the church of St. Blasius, close by the Cathedral, the Poljana (Meadows), here is Onofrije's Small Fountain, Orlando's Pillar, old Stanac. The play is *Novela od Stanca,* a pearl among Držić's comedies, a Renaissance srory where village and town, classes and vice meet.

The comedy *Tirena* is a forerunner of Gundulić's *Dubravka,* because for Marin Držić, and also for those who came after him, liberty was the most precous gift of nature.

The song of Tirena is the song of the legenday Arion, who came into Rijeka Dubrovačka riding on a dolphin and gave it its name. Dubravka takes from her breast the bagpipes and urges on Marin the poet: »Take them, and from now onwards play beside the river on the grass to the glory of Dubrovnik, the celebrated town.«

Wherever we turn, there is an artist or poet following us, this is a Town in which art determined history, Menčetić's flute follows us from Minčeta Tower, the most monumental fortress, because the poet knew that he must erect a bulwark to defend the liberty of his verse. Here is the window of Džore Držić, from which his lute sung out into the night and called the Morning Star and his passionate maiden.

Regardless of duty and origin, there were no differences among Dubrovnik poets, they lived their own lives, with worry or joy, overcome by catastrophe or when life was merciful, they took whatever it brought them. And that is why Dubrovnik poets still live today.

Remeta also comes out to meet us, his long sinnous shadow stretches from the islet of Sv. Andrija. The joyful and smiling word of Mavro Vetranović rings out like the cricket and sings of »wounded does«. Here is his street, house and doorway, although the 16th century is far away. From Crevljar, sv. Barbara, Vare, Ispodmirje, Izamirje, Peline, Prijeko, na Bokaru, Polača; the stages, the footsteps and eyes of Dubrovnik poets and rulers during the centuries are still alive in the streets.

Cvijeta Zuzorić filled Dubrovnik and Italy with admiration for her beauty and her verse. The Medici court in Florence was enchanted by this Dubrovnik poetess. Many wrote about her, and dedicated their verse to her, including Tasso:

> *»E certo quisto fior di alta bellezza*
> *E di virtu, che nell'Illiria nacque.«*

History and culture compete here to show this ancient town off as magnificently as possible. The Sponza Mansion, playfully Renaissance and meditatively Gothic, built by Paskoje Miličević, is a nucleus of Dubrovnik's historical culture. Today the Sponza houses one of the most voluminous European archives, the Dubrovnik Historical Archives, a treasure with thousands of volumes, chronicles and records, events, daily notes and news, diplomas and certificates, historical regulations enacted by the Senate, reports on the fleet, trade, schooling, wars,

natural disasters, the birth and death of citizens. In it is an enormous forest of manuscripts: about 7,000 hand-written books from the days of the Dubrovnik Republic, 100,000 individual documents, 1,000 oriental documents etc. The first records date from the first half of the 9th century, when heroic and fortified Dubrovnik defended itself from the Saracens and went through one and a half years of heavy siege. Orlando's Pillar bears witness to that historical victory for liberty and independence. The Archives include the Dubrovnik Annals. They are the most fundamental history of the Dubrovnik Republic. The first written records date from the 12th century, when the Dubrovnik Senate decided that the Annals should become a permanent record of historical documantation. The Ranjina family did much in compiling the first Annals. Anonymous persons wrote down all that was known about the town's history up to the 12th century, often making use of legend. Today the Dubrovnik Annals are written by experts of the Historical Institute in Lapad, in the lovely Renaissance Sorkočević Mansion, from whose family came many poets and great minds of Dubrovnik.

In the Sponza was also the famous Dubrovnik mint, the customs house, and goldsmith-filigree workshops.

The first literary *Academia dei Concordi* was also founded in the Sponza at the beginning of the 16th century by the writers Bobaljević, Monaldi, I. Getaldić, M. Menčetić, B. Tudisić, M. Kaboga and I. Ameltei. At the head of Dubrovnik's culture were poets, writers, scientists, humanists and Latinists, great men of the Renaissance, and many church orders.

Some Dubrovnik poets were crowned poets laureate in Rome as early as the middle of the 14th century: Petar M. Menčetić, Cervinus Tubero, Ilija Crijević - Aelius Lampridius Cerva. Crijević became poet laureate at 22 at the Literary Academy in Rome, led by the famous poet and humanist Pomponius Laetus. Crijević was one of the most educated humanists of Dubrovnik and Europe. In 1494 he was made Rector of the Dubrovnik School (situated in the Sponza Mansion) and headed it, with interruptions, until 1520. Under this genial poet Dubrovnik schooling reached European level.

The famous Italian and European humanist Ivan of Ravenna, pupil of Petrarca, writer of many humanistic works and of the history of Dubrovnik, today in the National Library in Paris, taught Dubrovnik pupils in the Sponza.

The Dubrovnik Archives hold the 1359 decisions of the Small Council concerning regulations on teachers' wages. In that period Dubrovnik youths, like their elders, had to be schooled and pay their own teachers. In 1435 the »Ordo consilii maioris« Council gave the title »Magistro in gramatica, retorica, loyca e filosofia« for »scolari e adulti e non adulti« to Filip de Diversis, and to Georgius Brugnolus the title »Magistro de scola gramatica positiva« for teaching commerce. Filip de Diversis was also Rector of the school from 1436-40. Dubrovnik teachers and rectors, the famous humanists Daniel Clarius of Parma and Demetrius Halkokondylas bear witness to the great care the Dubrovnik Republic took of the education of its citizens. In 1455 the law was passed that »anyone who cannot write or read canot serve the state« (Medini). The Dubrovnik Republic introduced a permanent notary service composed of four or five learned persons. Ser Bartholomeus de Sfondratis of Cremona served as notary in the Republic for a full 46 years. Ivan of Ravena was also notary in Dubrovnik from 1384 to 1387, and was paid 160 ducats and lodgings.

Dubrovnik is a town of libraries, almost every house has one, and so have public istitutions and monasteries. The 15th century library of Bishop Krušić of Trebinja has 2,000 volumes. They were bequeathed to the Dominican library, with the clause that »everyone must have access to the monastery libraries« and that »the books must be chained to the tables« so as not to be taken out and thus damaged.

During the famous Serafin Cervo the Dominican library had 10,000 volumes, many written on parchment. There were also many incunabula. In 1511 the Senate decided to give the Dominicans 300 perpers for a second time to organize a public library. The Library of St. Jacob of Višnjica was also extensive and old. In 1533 Sigismunds Phiochristus donated it 200 rare volumes. The most complete and best preserved library in the town is the Franciscan Library in the Monastery of the Little Brothers. Apart from many incunabula, it also possesses great works of Dubrovnik ecclesiastical literature, written in Latin on parchment in the 12th, 13th and 14th centuries. Here is also Marulić's first printed work Judita from 1526, and many other rarities of Dubrovnik 15th, 16th and 17th century literature.

Already in the 16th century Nikola M. Barna attempted to found a large commune library in Dubrovnik. Today there is such a historical library in the Rector's Palace, the Scholarly Library of Dubrovnik. It has a very old fund of books, including 150,000 volumes, 78 incunabula, 910 valuable manuscripts. It also includes all the books that used to belong to the Collegium Ragusinum Library. The Dubrovnik library is world famous and has been an invaluable historical and literary treasure through the centuries.

Dubrovnik is the birth town of one of the first European printers Bonino de Boninis, whose many printed works are in Dubrovnik, Venice, Rome and Florence, and can also be found in scholarly libraries and collections in the town and its neighbourhood. Today several incunabula of this great Dubrovnik printer are owned by the Bogišić Library in Cavtat, which possesses 22,000 volumes, 76 Slav incunabula, and over 1,000 letters of famous world personages. The Dubrovnik Archives record that in 1502 the priest Radovanović bequeathed to the priest Vukašinović a printing press (torculo da imprimere libri). Luka Primojević tried to found a large Dubrovnik printing house in 1514. There were several bookshops in the town, whose librari spread golden letters among the Dubrovnik reading public. The Dubrovnik Archives possess a very valuable 16th century document, a list of Renaissance and classical works which were sent from the Venetian printing house of Trajan Navo to the bookseller Antun de Odiolis in Dubrovnik. The list shows the great interest of the Dubrovnik public in a good Renaissance or classical book. Included on the list are: Ariosto, Tasso, Terenci, Boirdo, Ovid, Petrarca, Juvenal, Cicero, Pliny, Aretino, Virgil, Herodot, Homer, Dante, Hesoid, Xenophant, French realists, the 7th century physicians' book by Paul Eginjanin of Byzantium and others. Dubrovnik gave Europe the first books on trade, law, mathematics, physics, history, geography.

Beno Kotruljić wrote the famous work *Della mercatura e del mercante perfetto libri IV* (Four Volumes on Commerce and the Perfect Merchant). Crijević Tuberona wrote a work which caused a tempest in Europe because he attacked Popes Alexander VI, Julius II and Leo X.

Dubrovnik took its first revolutionary steps in poetry in the 15th and 16th centuries. It was the fiery baptism for the native language. The people of Dubrovnik, the metropolis of the Adriatic, the leader among Dalmatian-Croatian towns, began to use the native language for verse. Dubrovnik poetry was close to the people because of the unwritten rule that made people sing about or write down events. All that had to be remembered, notes, memories and legends of the Town, was written down or put into verse. Letters were penned on parchment, papyrus, canvas and leather in shaking but conscientious hands by poets, scribes, aided by friends, by men of the church, princes, members of the councils.

Anthologies and collections of poetry did not flourish in any town as they did in Dubrovnik. One of the first was the anthology of Nikša Ranjina containing 612 poems. There was a storm of applause for Ranjina when the anthology came out and flashed through Dubrovnik like a golden arrow. In it were to be found anonymous, folk and well-known writers: Džore Držić, Šiško Menčetić, Marin Krističević, Andrija Čubranović and others. There were also anthologies of poems by Marin Držić, Nikola Nalješković (16th century), Dinko Ranjina (16th century), Dominko Zlatarić (16th century). Their number is not known because everyone composed verse and everyone dedicated most of their poems to their much-loved town. More verse was certainly composed in this town than in any other in the history of mankind, thanks to the Dubrovnik Republic, which provided both freedom and material aid for poets. There were literary academies in the Sponza Mansion and Fort Revelin, also in many private homes of poets and scholars, and a »literary Arcadia« flourished in the Dubrovnik surroundings, the villages of the Dubrovnik coast, Rijeka, Župa and Konavli. On the Pelješac peninsula in Vručica was the summer house of Dinko Ranjina, a modest and joyful house, open to all for gatherings and literary conquests. Ranjina was a reviver of 16th century Dubrovnik literature. This was a golden century for the Croatian language, whose literature became part of European history. Ranjina was Rector of the Dubrovnik Republic seven times, merchant, ardent friend of the ordinary man and of the folk song. He left Dubrovnik indebted for golden centuries to come. He was a strong, conscientious, hard-working and moral Rector, an educated and talented poet, and he also wrote in Italian to show Europe the beauty of his homeland.

The poet Dinko Zlatarić stands together with Ranjina in Dubrovnik Renaissance poetry. Rector of the University of Padua at 21, he was also poet laureate. With his inhorn Dubrovnik skill at diplomacy he defended the building and honor of the university from armed rebels. As Rector, he stepped out unarmed before the town gates, calmed the rebels and parleyed with them.

There is still a memorial plaque in the hall of the university erected in honour of Rector Zlatarić. After that Zlatarić returned to Dubrovnik and remained there until his death in 1613. He also put the Town in his debt with his beautiful Renaissance poetry. »I learnt in the middle of glorious Dubrovnik, in which I was born, what the path of glory is«. He was member of many academies and societies, and lived for the good and glory of Dubrovnik, as did all the poets. It is not by chance that these patriotic and poetic verses are written above the door of Fort Lovrijenac: *Non bene pro toto libertas venditur auro* (Do not sell liberty for all the treasure in the world).

Dubrovnik had as many poetic circles as there were families. We shall mention only some: the Vetranović circle, the circles around Cvijeta Zuzorić, Marin Držić, the Crijević family, etc.

The old classical Greek and Latin cultures remained inexhaustible and tireless teachers of ideals, but they were not copied. Contemporary Italian Renaissance literature helped the Dubrovnik literary republic to show itself on its own fertile soil. Dante, Petrarca, Tasso and Ariosto were all known, but they were not simply remodelled. In the literary culture of any period and any nation, be it a narrow local one or wider, on the level of a state, even of the world, reciprocity is inevitable, as is fertilization from the same tree of humanistic literary heritage. The art of literature has no boundaries because the stronger the fertilization, the more authentic the literature.

Dubrovnik poetry bears all the characteristics of originality, typical marks of its native soil. It is the reflection of its own sun in the sea like Pirha, the silver and golden undulations of the Mediterranean, it is the hamonious silhouette of the Town, as touchable as the sea and the earth, as indispensible as air and water, bread and salt, love, wine and liberty. The spontaneity of the national spirit in folk song, prophecies and expressions, in dances, the *kolo* and verse games, in ceremonies, wedding songs and carnival songs, morning songs and serenades, in poems long and short, autobiographic or historical, ensure that. Dubrovnik literature will last many more centuries. The symbiosis of cultures, peoples and arts created here, on the rock of Ragusa, is a masterpiece to last through literary periods.

History passed below the Jesuit stairway, above which stands the church of St. Ignatius Guarding great and old art treasures. Facing it is Boškovićeva Poljana and the famous Collegium Ragusinum. Below, on today's Placa, a monument to Gundulić by Rendić (1893). Beside the poetic, tall and dignified figure are engraved four scenes from *Osman*: the Liberty of Dubrovnik; the Hermet Blasius, the patron of the Dubrovnik Republic; the imprisoned Sunčanica and her blind father, who was a fiddler; and the Polish Prince Vladislav and his slaughter of the Turks at Hoćim. Here also the poet Ivan F. Gundulić stands. Ionely sovereign of thought, the sky and the open seas, a Croatian, South Slav and European trumpet of poetry, Dubrovnik's sun-illuminted climax, the immortal creator of the epics: *Osman, Dubravka* and *Suze sina razmetnoga*. The first epic buried Turkey, the destroyer of antique and classical centres of culture, the second elevated and eternalized Dubrovnik liberty and the beauty of the Republic, the third gathered experience and justice from thousands of years of transience. All three magnificent epics are deep mirrors of Dubrovnik, reflecting generations and the universe. The realism of his lyrics provides a constant vision of events. »Kingdoms die, towns die / and are hidden by the grass,/ and because this life is mortal, / man is not at peace in his heart.« *(Suze sina razmetnoga)*. Pigeons still seem to repeat Dubravka's godlike hymn from the poet's shoulders: »Oh beautiful, sweet, cherished liberty ... / all silver, all gold, all human lives / canot pay your pure beauty.« You are like bread for the starving, happiness for the sorrowful, rest for the tired sailor after the shipwreck.

The paving underfoot seems to vibrate with the rivers of Gundulić's thought, waves beat against house that belonged to him in the 17th century. Here he walked, a spirited and rebellious boy, the furious poet of *Osman,* twice Rector in Konavli, a man more plebeian than noble, in love with the folk language and costume, simplicity and the human mind, the poet who made famous the Dubrovnik »Slav« language and cleared for it a path into literary Europe, who was for many years »*avvocato del proprio*« and »*Console dell cause civili*« of the Dubrovnik Republic. On the corner of Barbarska ulica (today Božidarevićeva) there is a three-storey house above whose stone doors are the coats of arms of Gundulić's family, a »horse's head« in a Renaissance-Gothic shield. That was long ago. This great poet was buried in the Franciscan church in 1638. Beside his grave hangs a stone wreath, the gift of his beloved Dubrovnik. On the votive plaque we seem to read: »Death looks at no man's face: it bears down alike on poor shacks and princely palaces.« *(Suze sina razmetnoga)*. In the Franciscan library are kept the oldest copies of Gundulić's *Osman* (from 1652 by Nikola Ohmučević of Dubrovnik), and the first printed copy of *Osman* in Dubrovnik (1862).

While Gundulić's 17th century trumpet still rings out, while it still calls warmly from below Mount Srđ, on the corner of Široka ulica and Stradun, the enthusiast and dreamer Ivo Vojnović peers out to hear it and fuse it into his tragedy. His modest house, his birthplace, whose green shutters open towards Stradun, have not forgotten that in 1857 one of the greatest sons of Dubrovnik was born here, and that he died far from the rock of his birth in 1929.

Dubrovnik and Vojnović are synonyms for the turning point in the battle of life, when liberty guarded for thousands of years was lost. After glorious centuries of freedom and great Dubrovnik poets, only bare life was left for Ivo Vojnović, a town taking its last breaths, the eternal and indestructable sea and the beloved rock. From afar he remembered its face and his native soil, nostalgia drew the life out of him, his spirit flew: »to the south, where giant rocks stand proud on the horizon, where vast open seas spread wherever you turn your eye, where the sky, translucent as a sapphire, spreads out and shines magnificently above the ruins of my Town«.

His tragedies were the intermezzos of his own life, medicine for the emptiness that came after the destruction of liberty, a kind of painful momentary comfort, breathing spaces on the road to eternity. Gundulić's prophetic vision foretold the tragedy of Dubrovnik. Vojnović's Promethian genius concealed a wounded heart full of love and gave it life through the ages. His *Lapad Sonnets* are like miraculous arcades, like a rain of thought falling into the deep and fertile soil. »Dusk fell. - The last rays of the setting sun followed Kalamot, spread out like a golden fan in the clear blueness of the evening sky. The sea slumbered calm, tired after the afternoon maestral, rolling lazy waves to the nearby shore ... Tired silence overflowed nature, broken only by the ceaseless lapping of the sea embracing the shore. Everywhere lingered the smell of the soil, full of the scent of myrtle and pine...«

Vojnović, with his pen, circled his native town, passing through the thousand-year-old streets, moving swiftly towards Bokar or below the walls of Sv. Marija, or sometimes circling around the heights of Bosanka, Žarkovica, Brgat and Šumet, the rocks and stoneslides of Orsula, around the Lazaret, sv. Jakob, through Konavli, by Posat, and then down again to Danče, Gradac, under Lovrijenac, Petka on Montovijerna and his beloved Mihajlo. What his unceasing devoted steps of love for his birth Town could not do, he did through the cosmos of thouhgt in his literary tragedies. His *Trilogy* is a master-piece of Croatian modern literature, one of the pearls of Dubrovnik literature. It eternized in a literary work the loss of liberty, and showed that in Dubrovnik's deepest agony and during her greatest suffering, the people still lived. Although Napoleon's troops roared through Dubrovnik abolishing the Republic in 1806, life went on. Instead of the flowering crowns of the Renaissance, Gundulić's and Palmotić's freedom-loving cloaks, Vojnović donned the toga of death and lamentation. That is why those three twigs of »laurel, wormwood and healther« grew, which the writer gave to his »dead father, so that they do not wilt in the shade of the cypress on Mihajlo«.

It is not by chance that Dubrovnik's thousand-year-old literary heritage embarked in the 20th century on the ship of Ivo Vojnović with such force, that others could hardly keep up. He was and remains the best creator of style in Croatian modern literature, and an unsurpassed portrayer of the human soul.

The modern critic Marijan Matković says about Vojnović: »Fate linked him, as it linked Titan, to the rocks of Dubrovnik's calm and cliffs, to the landscapes of Lapad and Gruž, the green of Petka and Lokrum, the murmur of the sea, the voices, scents and colours of his birthtown, its reality and its legend«. Let us hear, together with Vojnović, the revolt of Dubrovnik's inhabitants, princes and rulers, when they fell into slavery: »And if this thousand-year-old land of liberty must fall, and *we, homo!*... brothers, - children! Our ships are in the port. Let us board them and take the banner of St. Blasius, and let us sail away, like our ancient fathers! - oh joyful voyage!... *Homo! Homo!* Gulls and clouds will ask us - who are you? What are you seeking?... and the sails will answer. Dubrovnik sails! Dubrovnik seeks again a bare rock to hide Liberty.«

After Napoleon's troops others came to bury the liberty of the glorious Republic: Austria-Hungary, the dictatorship of old Yugoslavia, the terror of fascist occupiers and their collaborators. Until, in October 1944, the immortal Dubrovnik Republic was boen again, after 138 years of darkness, in the free Republic of Yugoslavia.

Through all those days the Sirens of Dubrovnik's sea lived on, scattering their moving song on the crags. It merged with the echo of Dubrovnik's fleet from the most furious depths of the seas. The freedom-loving spirits of the winds came out from the waves, their throats burning in the name of true life. And »an echo answered in song from the shore. The duet of the woods and the sea was dazzling!« (*Sirene,* Ivo Vojnović). Born in the deep centuries before humanism and the Renaissance, carefully guarded and nurtured in folk tradition, in event and legend, in song and story, stored in the heart of humanistic and Mediterranean centres, the creators of Dubrovnik literature were mature and able enough to express its master-pieces in the Croatian language even in the 15th and 16th centuries. That literature went out beyond the confines of Dubrovnik and of our homeland, and became part of the world's literary heritage. The peaks were Držić, Gundulić and Vojnović, but there were others also, the families of Mažibradić, Krstičević, Bunić, Palmotić, Gundulić (descendents of the great poet), Menčetić, Fučetić, Sorkočević, Lukarević, Rastić, Gradić, Ferić, Kaznačić, Kazali, Appendini, Orbini and many others. All together they created and forged the lierature of Dubrovnik. During the centuries their smithies throbbed with ringing and persistent literary truths. Today the town is rightly proud of them. Libraries, archives, schools and records, museums and galleries, anthologies and incunabula, private and public collections of many learned men of Dubrovnik, captains, princes an rulers are full of them. They can be found on portraits, in the houses of the writers of the Annals, of historians and scholars, chroniclers and painters of Dubrovnik, both tragedians and musicians, miraculous builders in word and in stone. They also fill the graves, where eternal messages of glory and fame have been carved. They have merged with the Dubrovnik sea and rocks, with the pounding waves from the open sea, the seamen and the gulls crying in a immortal voice the powerful song of literature.

Marija Novaković

Music in Dubrovnik

The oldest records of music in Dubrovnik date from the 11th to the 13th centuries. Some fragments of neuma codices came from other lands, but most are choral codices written in Dubrovnik scriptoria (27 in the Franciscan Little Brothers' Monastery, and 12 in the Dominican Monastery). Archives from 1302 mention the first town musician - the trumpeter Matej, and also eight more trumpeters, whose task it was to signal the beginning and end of work at work-sites around the town.

Music, of course, was part of church ceremonies, chiefly those in the Cathedral; during various ceremonies the *regens chori* of the Cathedral choir also conducted the Rector's chapel. It cannot as yet be established when the first organ was built in Dubrovnik, although it is mentioned in 1384. It is certain that in 1463 the Cathedral organist was a Slovene, Franciscus de Pavonibus, whose name is later joined by others.

In the 16th century at the latest, music began to become more and more important in the life of the town. At that time pastoral plays, comedies and tragedies of a secular character started to be shown together with miracle plays, and they were - according to notes in the texts - accompanied by music. Thus 1546 documents mention *Posvetilište Abrahamovo (Abraham's Sacrifice)* by Marin Držić (1508-1567), and in 1550 his comedy *Dundo Maroje (Uncle Maroje)*. There were many such performances. Another author was Nikola Nalješković (1510-1587).

Many details about the musical life of old Dubrovnik are conected with the holiday of St. Blasius, the town patron, whose holiday was always celebrated with much music and by many musicians. Historians have recorded that music was played both in the church and outside it. Psalms and antiphonies were sung by choirs, and the hymn of St. Blasius was sung figurally polyphonically. The *laudes (acclamationes)* were especially ceremonial. Instrumental groups, composed of local and foreign musicians *(pifferi, gnacharini, tubetae, tubicines, lautarii, cimbas, tympanistae)*, played at dances and games, which often developed into a kind of tournament.

Among churches, most music was played in the Franciscan Monastery, where both vocal and instrumental music was nurtured. Outstanding among the Croatian 16th century musicians in Dubrovnik are the Franciscan Gavro Temparičić (Pemparricius), the merchant and later priest Sekundo Brugnoli, the Dominican Benedikt Babić, Emanual Zlatarić, called *Sommus musicus,* Ante Tudrović, the Dominican Nikola Gaudencije Radojčić and others, and in the 17th century the Franciscan Fran Gučetić-Paprica and the Dominican Vinko Komnen, author of literary works and discussions.

Soon after its appearence in neighbouring Italy, the opera came to Dubrovnik. By the beginning of the 17th century Dubrovnik poets were translating Italian operatic librettos, and writing new ones in the same spirit. Thus Paško Primojević published in Venice his own version of *Euridice* by O. Rinuccini, one of the first operas to be written at all (it was performed in 1600 in Florence, music by J. Peri). Dubrovnik amateurs performed it only about a decade later. The poet Ivan Gundulić (1589-1638) must also be mentioned. He translated Rinucci's *Ariadne,* and his pastoral allegoric play *Dubravka* (1628) was performed accompanied by music. In 1629 Junij Palmotić (1607-1657) wrote *Atalanta,* a melodrama set to music, considered by some to be the first Slav opera ever written. There is no proof of this, because all documents were destroyed during the great Dubrovnik eathquake in 1667.

The town revived relatively quickly after the earthquake thanks to favourable economic and political conditions in the free Dubrovnik Republic. However, it did not reach the level of its greatest development, that of the 15th and 16th centuries. In the second half of the 18th century, however, an economic renewal and a new boom were gradually experienced, especially in seafaring and trade. This also enabled the greater development of artistic life. Proof of this is the appearance of the amateur-composer Luka Sorkočević (1734-1789), a Dubrovnik patrician, who regularly held musical concerts and academies in his home. His symphonies and other works show that at that time there were also excellent musicians in Dubrovnik, capable of playing them. Luka's son Antun (1775-1841) composed music too, and Elena Pucić-Sorkočević, the first woman composer in Croatia, was also a member of that familly. The famous violinist and composer Ivan Mane Jarnović (1745-1804) was born »beside the waters of Dubrovnik«. He was an important composer of violin concertos in the second half of the 18th century, known throughout Europe not only for his music, but also for his capricious nature. His performances in Paris, Berlin, Warsaw, Petrograd, Vienna, London and elsewhere attacted the attention of musical publishers, so that even in his lifetime his works were published in Paris, Lyon, Berlin, Offenbach, Vienna, Hamburg, London and Naples. Jarnović left behind him about twenty violin concertos in which he followed the example of Mozart, but also made some original contributions. For instance, he was the first to introduce into the violin concerto the romance, a slow movement, and after his stay in Russia also wrote movements in the rhythm of the polonaise calling them *Air russe, Rondo russe* etc. Jarnović also composed string quartets, violin duets, sonatas for the harpsichord and other works.

After the fall of the Dubrovnik Republic (1808) almost all cultural life died, so that only Italian operas *(stagione)* are mentioned in the 19th century, one of which was performed in 1864 at the opening of the new theatre, built by the Dubrovnik noble Luko Bundić-Bondo. Important dates in the first half of the 20th century are the first visit by the Zagreb Opera (1910) and the foundation of the Dubrovnik philharmonic 1925), which, in spite of being composed of amateurs, under the leadership of the conductor Josef Vlach Vruticki was a serious artistic influence.

From 1928 until his death the famous Polish composer Ludomir Rogowski (1881-1954) lived and worked in Dubrovnik.

After the liberation of Dubrovnik (1944) at last conditions ripened for unhindered musical development, so that by 1946 the professional Municipal Orchestra was founded, whose task it was to nurture the cultural and musical heritage of Dubrovnik and to introduce its public to Yougoslav music and musicians. Under the leadership of the conductors Krešimir Kovačević, Klaro Mizerita, Anton Nanut and Nikola Debelić, the Municipal Orchestra developed into an outstanding artistic body, as testified by many acknowledgements in Yugoslavia, and during tours in Europe, the U.S.A. and Canada.

Since the liberation there has been a Secondary Music School in Dubrovnik, and in 1968 the violin department of the Zagreb Musical Academy started work, and has had some outstanding results. The Radio Choir must also be mentioned among vocal groups, and the group for folk dances and songs *Linđo* has made a valuable contribution to presenting the folklore of the peoples of Yugoslavia. Outstanding in chamber music is the *Collegium Musicum Ragusinum* group.

The tradition of light music in Dubrovnik dates from Vlaho Paljetak (1893-1944). He composed tunes which excellently conjure up the local colour of Dubrovnik. He also managed to present the atmosphere of the Hrvatsko zagorje region in his popular *kajkavski* songs. Several composers of light music later followed in his footsteps. The vocal-instrumental group the *Dubrovnik Troubadours* have acquired fame on tours far outside Yugoslavia.

Krešimir Kovačević

Natural and Medical Sciences

The greatness and beauty of the works of art of a region or a nation are only one way in which it lives on through history. Another dimension of historical permanence is provided by man's efforts to understand the world around him. The symbiosis of those two aspects of one single process are reflected in Dubrovnik. The people wanted to make their town richer in material goods, and this was reflected in their desire to make it more beautiful. Economic security and municipal development, which ran in peace in spite of all external problems, favoured the ambitions to understand the new and the unknown. One aspect of this was an interest in the natural sciences. The second, also very important, was the application of such sciences in the everyday life of the town and the many activities that went on in it.

The natural sciences were important in Dubrovnik's humanistically organized schooling system. Mathematics and physics were not taught in any depth in schools until the end of the 18th century. However, this did not stop the inhabitants of Dubrovnik from studying abroad. Some returned to their hometown and continued their work there, while others remained abroad and fought for their place in the world of science, showing the strength of the town which nurtured its talents by sending them abroad.

Ivan Gazulić, an astronomer and astrologer, worked in 15th century Renaissance Dubrovnik. Although much is not known about him, we do know that he kept in scientific contact with the at that time very highly developed cultural circles around the Croato-Hungarian King Matthias Corvinus in Hungary.

There is much information about people in 15th and 16th century Dubrovnik. There were many mathematicians and physicists. we shall mention some by name: Ludovik Crijević-Tuberon (1459-1527), the writer Mavro Vetranić (1482-1576), Grgur Budislavić-Natali (about 1500 - about 1550). There were also two others, whose work and activities we know more about.

The first was Nikola Gučetić (1549-1610). He wrote about problems in aesthetics, sociology and pedagogy, but one of his most important works is *Sopra le metheore d'Aristotile,* which is a commentary on Aristotle's work on meteorites. In connection with his studies on winds he took as examples two caves close to Dubrovnik, in Popovo, and Šipun cave in Cavtat.

Nikola Nalješković (before 1510-1587) was the leading Dubrovnik astronomer of his day. Records show that he possessed astronomic instruments. In 1579 his work *Dialogo sopra la sfera del mondo* was published in Venice. Although of no great theoretic value, Nalješković's practical contributions to the determination of the position of the pole and of so-called climatic regions are important. We know that Nalješković's opinion was sought during the reform of the calender carried out by Pope Gregory XIII. The practical results of the interest Dubrovnik took in the natural sciences can be seen in the work of Nikola Sagroević (d. 1573). He studied the problem determining the height of the tides in many European Atlantic ports, starting with Gibraltar.

In the middle of the 17th century Marin Getaldić returned to Dubrovnik, after spending many years travelling abroad. Getaldić was the first great mathematician and physicist in the real sense of the word. In his seven published books he treated many mathematical and physical problems, some of which were important contributions to the science of his time. He also made optical experiments, and in his cave in Ploče (»Beta's Cave«) experimented with converging mirrors.

Many inhabitants of Dubrovnik were also active in the sciences outside their homeland. Thus Juraj Dubrovčanin (Georgius Raguseus - 1579 - 1622) taught philosophy, mathematics and medicine at the University of Padua from 1601 onwards. His polemics, in which he strongly attacked astrology and various kinds of magic, are important.

Stjepan Gradić (1613-1683) lived in Rome for many years, and in 1682 he became curator of the Vatican Library. As a prominent member of the circle of scientists around the Swedish Queen Christina and Pope Alexander VII, he discusses with his contemporaries all the current scientific problems of those days.

The greatest Dubrovnik name in the history of the natural sciences is quite certainly that of Rugjer Josip Bošković (1711-1787). He was one of the greatest universal minds of his time, and of any time. It is almost impossible to list all the branches of science he was intensely engaged in. He was a mathematician who applied the law of continuity to various mathematical problems; a physicist who wrote a discussion on living forces, basic in his day; a geodetist who measured the angle between Rome and Rimini, making a valuable contribution to the determination of the shape of the Earth; an optician who discovered many new optical instruments; a technician who gave instructions for the building of a harbour, for draining the Pontine Marshes and repairing the dome of the Imperial Library in Vienna; an archeologist who was one of the first to study the problems of Augustus' Obelisk, Troy etc.

Bošković crowned his great and universal knowledge of the natural sciences with the syntheses *Theoria philosophiae naturalis redacta ad unicam legam virium in natura existentium* (1758), which gave him the name of a great scientist, and no less a philosopher. In that work he presented his dynamic atomic theory of matter, which is still of interest today in the modern study of atoms. We must also add that the famous physicists M. Faraday and lord Kelvin agreed with Bošković's conception concerning the atom as the centre of force.

Bošković and his work marked the end of the period of development of materialism and natural philosophy in the 18th century, and in many practical and theoretic elements they became universal.

Although there were no great and important names in 18th century Dubrovnik, a new quality then appeared. In 1777 the Piarist order took over teaching in schools. They wanted to introduce the natural sciences into the schooling system, and in 1787 were successful. From then on mathematics, physics and astronomy were taught systematically. Thus systematic schooling and the preparation for work in the natural sciences started.

The other great branch of the natural sciences in which Dubrovnik achieved great results both in the Republic itself and beyond it were medicine and pharmacology. Their development was influenced by many problems of public health, whose solutions were of vital importance for the Republic. Widespread commercial connections and the port itself were a constant danger for the spreading of infections and many other diseases, and the problem of preventing and fighting them was always present.

Dubrovnik started solving public health problems very early.

In its first law, the 1272 Statutes, we find the beginning of some medical, social and public-health measures of public importance. Those were regulations on street cleaning, prohibitions on discarding garbage, etc. Other questions of public health were regulated by numerous later regulations: sewage is mentioned in 1395; in 1336 and 1398 keeping animals in the town was prohibited; in 1328 the street paving started; and in 1415 a permanent street-cleaning service was established. In 1436-1438, 11,700 metres of piped water were installed.

Besides for measures to protect health in general, Dubrovnik very early took measures for the direst struggle against disease. In 1347 the town hospital *Domus Christi* was opened. In 1540 it was turned into the first public hospital with a permanent medical staff regulated by special instructions. The statute contained very modern regulations in 13 articles. The doctors were obliged to visit the hospital patients in the morning and evening. The hospital had its administration and supervisors, nurses, and also a hospital pharmacy. No greater changes took place until the fall of the Republic, when the hospital had 6 doctors and several barber-surgeons.

They succeeded each other in carrying out the duties of the *ordinarius* and assistant doctor. All this shows that over 400 years ago the hospital was organized in a modern way. We must also add that in 1451 the Republic founded a hospital as part of its consulate in Constantinople, to be used by its consuls and other Dubrovnik citizens there.

A very progressive and interesting institution was the Dubrovnik orphanage, which cared for abandoned (mostly illegitimate) children. It was founded in the Convent of St. Claire, probably quite soon after the foundation of the Convent itself (1290). On February 9, 1432, the Republic founded the *Ospedale dell misericordia* orphanage and drew up a special statute. In comparison we must add that an orphanage was founded in Paris in 1636, in Moscow and Petrograd 100 years later, and in Vienna in 1784.

Contagious diseases were a great danger in old Dubrovnik, and measures to prevent them date from the distant past. In 1320 a leper-house for the isolation of lepers is mentioned in Pile. The method of isolating passengers suspected of carrying a contagious disease was very early seen to be correct in Dubrovnik. Regulations of July 27, 1377, required that all comers from suspect regions must spend a month in quarantine in special places (first in Cavtat, on Mrkan, Bobara and Sv. Petar). In 1590 the Lazaret in Ploče (which still exists) gradually started being built. Regulations for the Lazaret were very strict and rigourously kept to prevent the mixing of the healthy and the diseased. In 1426 special persons, the *kacamorti* (from *cacciatore* = hunter, *morti* the dead, the hunter of death, *Todesjeger)* were employed there. They had the final word in the public prevention of disease. If disease appeared in any part of the Republic the region was sealed off, and exit and entry were forbidden.

Pharmacists and pharmacies were also essential for the struggle against disease, not only doctors and hospitals.

Records from 1293 mention the first pharmacist. But an especially important year is 1317, when the pharmacy of the Little Brothers was founded. It was the first pharmacy, and is today the oldest pharmacy in Europe still to be working (two later ones were founded in Hildesheim in Germany in 1318 and 1341).

Besides founding medical institutions, the inhabitants of Dubrovnik also paid attention to the employment of professional doctors and pharmacists. The first doctor is mentioned in Dubrovnik in 1280 (until then barbers worked as doctors). There were two kinds of doctor. One group had graduated from medical faculties, the other, pupils of surgeons'

schools, undertook surgery, obstetrics, removal of stones and similar activities. The Republic always tried to have at least one doctor and one surgeon, and after 1440 two.

Many important doctors and pharmacists who worked either in the Republic or abroad came from Dubrovnik. Besides the two most famous, Dominik Dubrovčanin (Domenico de Ragusa) and Gjuro Baglivi, who were only born in Dubrovnik and spent their whole lives abroad, there were also many others. During his studies in 1570 Dominko Zlatarić was Rector of the University of Padua. Although he was not a doctor, he reintroduced the teaching of practical medicine in that university. Luka Stulli (1772-1828) was made commune doctor in 1799. In 1801 he introduced vaccination against smallpox according to a method recommended to him by Edward Jenner three years earlier. He even published a special booklet on the subject, with instructions in Croatian and Italian (1805). We must add that in 1847 the Dubrovnik doctors Niko Pinelli and Frane Lopišić carried out an operation using ether as anesthetic. Since the first operation using ether as an anesthetic was carried out by John Collins Ward in Boston on October 16, 1846, then this is certainly one of the first cases in Europe, quite certainly in Yugoslavia.

Finally, we must add that one of the most famous doctors of his time, the Portuguese Jew Amatus Lusitanus (1511-1568), spent a short time in Dubrovnik. In his great work *Curationum medicinalium centuriae septem* he described 100 cases from his Dubrovnik practice in 1556-1558.

Through this short survey of the development of the natural sciences in Dubrovnik, we can freely say that Dubrovnik, in spite of many circumstances which hindered the free development of science (constant struggles for the preservation of independence, the care to preserve commercial and economic connections, the lack of higher education, etc.), achieved an enviable level in the natural sciences and medicine, and through its sons who were active abroad, it made an important contribution to the scientific history of mankind.

Mirko Kratofil

A White Town of Stone

»*Were there more than one Dubrovnik in the world, only one would be real - that true, authentic and only Dubrovnik of stone and light. That palm held open under the stars, offered to the world; a unique stage where past and future have a common meaning, their own creative measure ...*

Dubrovnik is not only a work of art. Through the long centuries it has also been a creator. Exposed to outside influence, but always its own. Turned to the winds, but always firm and unyielding.

Human thought and the spirit of liberty kept watch on its stone towers and walls, not the might of arms. Dubrovnik was not made great through victories wrought with the sword, but through the strength of creative inventivity.. Dubrovnik is a town of poets and a poet-town ...«

Jure Kaštelan

Is any town in the Southern Adriatic as well known for its beauty as is Dubrovnik, the most important Yugoslav historical, cultural and tourist centre? According to the latest data, this white town of stone probably grew up in the first centuries A.D. Always, like today, its freedom-loving spirit linked the past with the present in the atmosphere of the warm Mediterranean climate.

Thanks to its geographical position, its historical role during the centuries and the harmony of its natural and social facets, today Dubrovnik has built up its own image that makes it stand out from other Adriatic tourist towns and regions. This image has also made it unique among the tourist-resort towns of Europe.

Dubrovnik is the regional, political and cultural centre of Southern Dalmatia. Its wider region includes the narrow coastal strip stretching from Neum-Klek to Oštro promontory at the entrance to the Gulf of Kotor. It includes the Elaphite Islands, Mljet, Korčula, Lastovo and Pelješac Peninsula.

Dubrovnik is a rich treasury of architectural styles of the past. Its monuments of culture are priceless, always carefully guarded, and especially in new socialist Yugoslavia. Thus it is no wonder that this town, with its outstanding century-old monuments of highest degree, has been included in UNESCO's register of the cultural heritage of the world. The citizens of Dubrovnik knew so well, firmly and harmoniously how to build and root into their own soil the cultural heritage of their town. This can be felt in their customs, their consciousness, their mentality and in all the events of public and economic life, and it filled the whole world with admiration. Dubrovnik's heritage was built up during long centuries of life in freedom. It takes many different forms, and can be found in archives, libraries and institutions full of documents from Dubrovnik's past, in its own literature and works of art from so many periods.

Dubrovnik's cultural heritage is built into its walls and towers, its ancient buildings, churches and monasteries, its squares and streets, patrician summer-houses standing in tame and shady gardens, in its customs, way of life and the consciousness of its citizens. Everything we encouter was carefully nurtured for centuries and harmonized into a unique balance between nature and the products of the human spirit.

Dubrovnik has recently become the metropolis of Yugoslav tourism. Every year about 700 thousand Yugoslav and foreign guests visit its riviera and realize over five million tourist nights. Its mild climate, lovely countryside and historical-cultural heritage, together with all that was done here in the post-war period, have made Dubrovnik Yugoslavia's window into the world. Crucial for its further development and its high-quality off-season tourist offer was the integration of culture, cultural events and the total cultural life of Dubrovnik into the tourist offer of its hotels and restaurants, and also its crafts, traffic and retail offer. All this together adds up to what the modern tourist can chose from when he visits Dubrovnik.

There is nothing specific about Dubrovnik's favourable climate or its communications possibilities, its lovely beaches or its outstanding bathing, or about its sports grounds. The only thing that is specific for the Dubrovnik environment is its cultural heritage and its existing forms of cultural life and activities.

This fact, and also the fact that culture has been integrated into the main economic activity of the town, tourism, has enabled the very successful material symbiosis between tourism and cultural activities.

A careful traveller must notice that the marvelous harmony of this town is not only a question of form, but also stems from its deepest spiritual content. Here harmony is not only the result of the good taste of its citizens or of the craftskill of its builders. It is something more: through a long series of centuries, harmony was the condition for Dubrovnik's survival as a town, as a republic, the condition of its freedom.

That is why we see in Dubrovnik one of the forces of our spiritual homeland. And that is certainly why every tourist in Dubrovnik has gone through a moment when he thought that he should at last unpack his cases and say to himself: I have arrived!

The Dubrovnik Summer Festival

Dubrovnik was not chosen in 1950 for the centre of a new Yugoslav theatre event by chance. All its rich history - material and spiritual - contributed to this choice. Not only the harmony of its architecture and its urban spaces, and even less its tourist attraction, which was in any case not so internationally important in 1950. What came first was all that we call the soul of a town. Its special light. The magnetism of what is its own. Its radiance. The reason for this choice was Dubrovnik's long history.

In 1950 a lovely idea was born in Dubrovnik, the idea to organize a Dubrovnik Festival and thus revive the rich tradition of the Renaissance theatre and revitalize the monumental environment of the town.

This was the answer to the question: what is the place and role of Dubrovnik, should it be left to vegetate proud of its history, or should a way be found in New Yugoslavia for it to set sail again with full sails.

In this town, which is at the same time history and museum and unique theatre stage, but primarily life itself, the Dubrovnik Summer Festival started. Dubrovnik was the first in Yugoslavia to have a literary language, it was the site of the first successes in all the fields of art, it imposed itself with all its inner strength. Dubrovnik opened its doors to all the works whose artistic power overcame time and space. It has become a cultural focus and the place where all the most eminent artists and companies in Yugoslavia meet, a place where Yugoslavia meets the world.

Is this town a miracle or an anachronism, man's yearning or his retreat, the last act of the Dubrovnik Republic or the beginning of a new chapter?

It remained a town open to art. It proves that theatre - the temple of Thalia - still has an audience spiritually ready to accept and experience it.

And that is what makes it unique.

Dubrovnik is thus linked with and responsible to its past, beauty and tradition. Every staging mounted here is already »pre-directed« by the environment. Real blocks of stone, the true magnificence of rock and the power of vaults, real pines, a real fountain or well and real balconies, quite understandably, offer the spectator more than do theatre props.

The stage, the scenery of the play and the site that it takes place on, sometimes takes up more of the audience's attention and impresses itself more sharply than the play itself.

In a town in which every stone is worn away by the steps of so many generations that lived, suffered, loved, hoped and died, artistic and cultural life throbs passionately. Thirty or forty years may not be much in the history of a people or of a town, but the thirty or forty years of the Festival mean a lot in the history of post-war Dubrovnik, in the development of the Yugoslav national culture, in integrating the creativity of all its peoples, in its penetration into the world. Finally, they mean a lot in the life of those many participants and organizers who grew and matured together with the Festival. One of the most famous centres of the Slav Renaissance, which in the 16th century competed in wealth and power with the Florence of the Medicis, Dubrovnik is a town whose every corner holds countless memories that recall many unexpected associations. Those associations, combined with characteristic architecture, guve a special colour to plays in which living reality is closely intertwined with romance and poetry.

The town's external form and its history play a great part in deciding on the Festival's repertoire. The Dubrovnik Summer Festival can rightly be called a holiday of poetry under the open sky. Comedies and pastoral plays by Gundulić, Držić and Lucić are played in the same environment in which their writers wrote and their heroes lived. Marin Držić, the famous Croatian comedy-writer, chose the square in front of Sponza Palace and Onofri's Fountain, as the site of his carneval comedy *Novela od Stanca*. It is completely natural, therefore, that four centuries later that same Placa should serve as a stage for actors in the same play. The mischievous pranks of Pomet and Petrunjela in *Dundo Maroje* are staged on the same sun-drenched meadow where the author of the comedy, Marin Držić, used to walk. To turn a whole town into a theatre is a great and imposing task both for its organizers and for its aritsts. The art of directing, to use all the possibilities offered by a natural environment to build up a living ambience, seems to have got its real essential dimension in Dubrovnik.

The history of the Dubrovnik Festival is also the history of the many stages in this magical town.

In a way completely its own, different from that in of any other festival town, Dubrovnik presents itself to the world as a theatre-town with a great many outdoor stages.

A special festival atmosphere permeates the whole old town, an atmosphere felt in the unity of man and his environment, of past and present, an atmosphere of the total essence of this town ennobled by history, nature and beauty.

Theatre performances, dramatic and musical, and also concerts and recitals, fit functionally into the architectural and natural stages, which thus become their original and natural setting.

This has resulted in performances that are authentic and characteristic of Dubrovnik, performances that grew up on a specially chosen and open stage, and that cannot be transferred to any other place because they would then lose their artistic originality.

Although an outdoor stage was built for the first festival, soon the natural and architectural areas of the old town began to be used for plays and musical performances, especially those that were written in Dubrovnik and in similar Mediterranean environments. This became one of the specific features of the Festival. Dubrovnik's gardens, porches, atriums and squares are no more than lovely sets. But even more important than the harmonious beauty of a stage are its acoustic properties and its size. These are the demands that decide whether a performance will be held out of doors or indoors (for instance, in one of Dubrovnik's churches).

But in the selection and in the performance of the extensive musical-theatre programme of the Dubrovnik Summer Festival the town obviously plays an important role not only as a harmonious stone setting with a rich past, but also as the fruitful synthesis of an ancient artistic tradition.

Sometimes the acoustics of a performance may not be ideal in the architecturally intricate atriums of old town mansions, on stone squares and in old Dubrovnik churches. But nevertheless, all this is lost before the subjective experience of the audience, which is always excited and enthusiastic about the meeting of sound and lovely Mediterranean forms.

The Dubrovnik Summer Festival is still a marvelous, changing stage, whose setting are the architecture, plant life and sky of an ancient, unique town. Plays are rarely brought here already finished, they are usually specially created for Dubrovnik. The Festival repertoire is not routinely composed of what has already been seen on other stages. More or less determined by the surroundings, it is always a surprise and a new discovery.

When we read the programme of the Dubrovnik Summer Festival, the very names of Dubrovnik's many natural stages are unusual: Gundulić Meadow, the Atrium of the Rector's Palace, Gradac Park, In Front of the Cathedral, Dominican Atrium, Franciscan Monastery, Držić Meadow, Fort Lovrijenac, Music-School Park, Fort Revelin, Lazaret, Gundulić Summer House, the Santa Marija. All these are not the names of theatres or music halls. There is no treatre in the usual sense in Dubrovnik in the summer, no sets, no curtains, no movable stages with props. During the Festival the whole town becomes a big stage.

The town seems to be populated by people of different ages, races, languages and beliefs, people who seem to be linked or who could be linked into a spiritual brotherhood by the common purpose that made them walk through Dubrovnik's widely open gates, whose keys are held by the theatre.

At the Festival artists and companies present to the Yugoslav and foreign audience the artistic achievements of the peoples of Yugoslavia, their cultural heritage and modern productive and reproductive creativity, on a very high level. Thus they contribute to fundamental research into the Croatian and Yugoslav heritage, bring it closer to the modern spectator, test their level of achievement before an international audience, enable an artistic break-through both to individuals and to cultural environments. Through unselfish efforts with a common purpose they create conditions for the integration of the cultures of all the Yugoslav peoples and nationalities and its penetration into the creativity of other nations.

The Dubrovnik Summer Festival is a specific and unique cultural event of the peoples and nationalities of Yugoslavia of international renown, whose origin and seat is Dubrovnik. It is a Yugoslav culture and art event, which has hosted the most eminent Yugoslav artists and companies. For many years now the Yugoslav and foreign audience has been watching the greatest artistic achievements of the peoples of Yugoslavia, their rich cultural heritage and modern creativity. The international character of the Festival was achieved through the high level of the performances, through engaging the best foreign companies and individual artisits, through the Festival audience, and especially through the repertoire, which includes world-famous works from all nations and was the force that gathered artists regadless of language and nation. Dubrovnik is an exceptional town, a recognized world stage. And this is especially important because of Yugoslavia's renown and its efforts to achieve peaceful cooperation among nations and countries, and the freedom of artistic creativity.

The Festival has been held every year since 1950 from July 10 to August 25, on the architectural and natural stages of Dubrovnik. During 47 days there are one, two and sometimes more performances every evening: plays, operas, ballets, symphony and chamber concerts, recitals or choir singing, and the folklore of the peoples and nationalities of Yugoslavia.

Besides its cultural importance, the Dubrovnik Summer Festival is also an important tourist attraction. It has greatly increased the tourist traffic in Dubrovnik and its surroundings.

The modern age has complemented Dubrovnik's rich history in an exceptionally suitable manner: through the art of the best masters of the stage and music world. Here, on the source of the past, is also the best place for us to get acquainted with each other and to introduce ourselves to the world.

The Festival is three-and-a-half decades of fantasy, reborn every summer in new form and new feverish imagination, searching and self-acknowledgement. Three-and-a-half decades of plays for which a whole ancient town is both an enchanted stage and a determinant and challenge. And an open invitation that knows no limits. An invitation to ancient but ever new plays on words, acting, sound, movement, colour ... Thousands of victories, thrills, rapture, bitter disapointment, rises and falls into a forest of applause, always under the same, shimmering summer stars above the white, stone town.

And so, from summer to summer. And so it will go on for many, many more years to come.

Who can count all the July and August nights of the Dubrovnik Summer Festival, starting with that long-past 1950 when it took many long hours to reach the town under Mt. Srđ travelling in black and sooty carriages across the war-torn and burnt-out Bosna or Lika. Where are the distant days when this aritistic adventure began, this adventure born not only by a happy chance, but also from the dreams and enthusiasm of many people today already forgotten: it was born and grew up on the squares, streets, gardens, courtyards, terraces and parks of Renaissance-baroque Dubrovnik.

Yes, what took place in that distant year really was the beginning of a magical Festival. It was also the beginning of the understanding and love a whole town showed for that Festival. Because without that understanding and love, without Dubrovnik's hospitality, the Festival would already long be dead. That chain of long Dubrovnik summer nights of acting, movement, music and words would have snapped. Because there are some kinds of art that cannot live even for a moment without atmosphere. An atmosphere created by living people, more than by the most enchanted stages. People open to the magic of art.

This flowering plant must grow into a strong tree with a rich crown under which all the people of the world can gather. The Dubrovnik Summer Festival has shown that it is not only stone, sun and sea - it is also man, his creative spirit. It is not only history with its eventful past - it is the living present, the fertile fermentation of the future.

And to conclude: the basic feature of the Dubrovnik Summer Festival today is that it is open to every authentic expression of human drama and human disquiet. Dreams sail under the flag of Libertas, from season to season, the drems of Yugoslav and foreign artists. Brought to life during Dubrovnik summer nights, they are not only a wonderful cultural experience, but also important documents of human solidarity. Because, however interesting the esthetic questions that guide, from season to season, the Dubrovnik Summer Festival towards an increasingly open and free world stage, they are all secondary before the fact that a miracle took place in this unique Yugoslav, Croatian, Adriatic town with a rich and celebrated past famous for the highly-developed sense of its inhabitants for whant is beautiful. From the dreams of poets and from romantic enthusiasm a stage for a great imaginative Festival was created - reborn like the Phoenix every summer. It shows the indestructable energy of all the peoples of Tito's socialist Yugoslavia, for which Dubrovnik has become a widely open, cultural and artistic window into the world. And not only a window, but also a heart on an open palm.

Tomo Vlahutin